"*Dream Interpretation for Beginners* shows the reader how to tap into the deeper meaning of a dream and inspires you to put that new insight to creative use in daily living. This book will instantly stimulate the reader."

—Bernie Ashman, author of *Intuition and Your Sun Sign*

"[This book] explains how your conscious and subconscious minds work together to create your own unique blend of imagery and symbolism ... I recommend *Dream Interpretation for Beginners* for anyone seeking the answers in their dreams."

—Sheila Englehart, author of *Warning Signs*

D1531011

Dream Interpretation
for Beginners

©Keith Papke

About the Author

Diane Brandon has been an Integrative Intuitive Counselor since 1992 and has interpreted others' dreams and studied sleep and dream research since the early 1970s. She views dreams as a wonderful tool for personal unfolding and insight, as well as for life enrichment and spirituality. She teaches classes and seminars on dreams, intuition, personal empowerment, creativity, and listening skills, in addition to wellness classes, and offers corporate consulting.

Diane is the author of *Invisible Blueprints: Intuitive Insights for Fulfillment in Life* and *Intuition for Beginners: Easy Ways to Awaken Your Natural Abilities*, as well as a contributing author to *The Long Way Around* and *Speaking Out*. Her private work with clients focuses on facilitating personal development and life fulfillment, and she brings other modalities into her work, such as dream work, guided meditation, regression, and Natural Process healing.

She has produced three meditation CDs, including *A Journey Within Meditation*, *Natural Process Healing*, and *Brainstorm in the Boardroom with Great Leaders*. She hosted a radio show, *Naturally Vibrant Living*, and is also a professional actor, singer, and voice-over artist. Born and raised in New Orleans, she has an A.B. from Duke University and did master's work at the University of North Carolina, in addition to French studies in Geneva, Switzerland.

Dream Interpretation

For Beginners

Understand the Wisdom of Your Sleeping Mind

DIANE BRANDON

Llewellyn Publications
Woodbury, Minnesota

FIRST EDITION
First Printing, 2015

Cover art: iStockphoto.com/21597474/© szefei,
        iStockphoto.com/20725748/©Ann_Mei
Cover design by Ellen Lawson

Llewellyn Publications is a registered trademark of Llewellyn Worldwide Ltd.

Library of Congress Cataloging-in-Publication Data
Brandon, Diane, 1948–
  Dream interpretation for beginners : understand the wisdom of your sleeping mind / by Diane Brandon. — First Edition.
    pages cm
  Includes bibliographical references.
  ISBN 978-0-7387-4191-8
1. Dream interpretation—Miscellanea. 2. Dreams—Miscellanea. I. Title.
  BF1078.B625 2015
  154.6'3—dc23
                    2014041441

Llewellyn Worldwide Ltd. does not participate in, endorse, or have any authority or responsibility concerning private business transactions between our authors and the public.
  All mail addressed to the author is forwarded, but the publisher cannot, unless specifically instructed by the author, give out an address or phone number.
  Any Internet references contained in this work are current at publication time, but the publisher cannot guarantee that a specific location will continue to be maintained. Please refer to the publisher's website for links to authors' websites and other sources.

Llewellyn Publications
A Division of Llewellyn Worldwide Ltd.
2143 Wooddale Drive
Woodbury, MN 55125-2989
www.llewellyn.com

Printed in the United States of America

Other Books by Diane Brandon

Intuition for Beginners: Easy Ways to
Awaken Your Natural Abilities
(Llewellyn Publications, 2013)

Invisible Blueprints:
Intuitive Insights for Fulfillment in Life
(Insight Publishing, 2005)

Contributing Author to:

Speaking Out
(Insight Publishing, 2005)

The Long Way Around:
How 34 Women Found the Lives They Love
(Carolina Women's Press, 2000)

Dedication

This book is dedicated to all the dreamers, those who strive to understand their dreams and use them as a tool for unfolding in their lives and who value the glimpses into other worlds, inner terrain, and spiritual realms that they can give us.

Acknowledgments

Every book represents the culmination of a tremendous amount of work and effort—and not just on the part of the author. This book is no exception. There are many people who have contributed to this book becoming a reality, and I am in their debt.

Thanks to everyone at Llewellyn who has worked to make this book a reality. Angela Wix has always been welcoming and open to whatever questions and materials I send her way, as well as easy to work with and prompt in responding to my numerous and seemingly endless questions. I worked closely with Andrea Neff, who served as production editor on this book, and would like to thank her for her assistance.

I would especially like to express gratitude to all those who contributed dreams for me to include with interpretations in this book. Some of these wonderfully cooperative people don't know me well, aside from my presence in my dream group on Facebook, yet many of them immediately replied to my plea for dreams. Others are close friends who willingly stopped what they were doing to send some of their dreams to me for inclusion. A book on dreams would be meaningless without dream samples in it, so I am indebted to all those who were kind enough to comply and "feed" me their dreams.

I would also especially like to thank Theresa Waltermeyer, who first started urging me in the mid-1990s to write a book on dreams, so taken was she by her perception of my ability to interpret dreams. She continued to exhort me, at seemingly regular intervals, to "write that book on dreams." The regular drumbeat of her promptings finally took hold, and I sat down in early 2013 to begin work on this book. Thanks, Theresa, for your persistent and knowing urgings! I hope this book meets your expectations and is the book you envisioned me writing.

I would also like to thank all the prodigious scientists who have researched our world of sleep and dreams over the years. Their research findings have shed valuable light on this other world of ours, and I am immensely grateful for their work and contributions to our knowledge and understanding. I started voraciously reading what I could find in this field of research back in the early 1970s, and to this day I still light up when I find new research findings. Researchers may not know those who read of their work, but many of us greatly appreciate their efforts.

Lastly, I would like to thank you, the reader, for having taken the time to access this book and read it. May it give you useful information and insight and be a tool for your life enrichment!

contents

Part 2: How to Interpret and Understand Your Dreams

Chapter 5: Tips for Interpreting Your Dreams and a Step-by-Step Procedure — 89

introduction

You startle awake, the traces of a dream dancing around the edges of your mind—persistent yet elusive. Scenes and faces leap out at you and then vanish, tantalizing you with their inconstancy, while emotions flicker and appear and disappear repeatedly. *What in the world was that about?* you wonder.

You may or may not be able to get the dream traces out of your mind. Some vestiges may linger and then evaporate, seemingly daring you to make sense of them. *It was so bizarre,* you keep thinking. *Since it was so bizarre, it couldn't mean anything,* you tell yourself.

Or could it?

Have you ever experienced this? If you have, then you're definitely not alone. Millions of people experience this almost nightly and have a similar reaction: *That dream was so bizarre. How could it possibly mean anything?*

Why do we have bizarre dreams? Could you learn to understand them? If you could understand them, would that help you in any way?

Welcome to the world of dreams, your "other world"! There's a lot to explore in your world of dreams, and my goal is to help you learn to understand this world.

I've been fascinated by dreams for many, many years now. I started interpreting dreams and reading everything I could find on sleep and dream research in the early 1970s. In my work as an Integrative Intuitive Counselor, I frequently interpret my clients' dreams and help them see the insight their dreams are giving them.

Dreams can make sense and offer more to us than they may seem to be able to do on the surface. They can hint at unseen riches lying beneath the surface within us. And we can begin to grasp and see what those riches are, as well as reclaim and use them for our own benefit, to enrich our lives and improve our relationships.

What lies in the way of us being able to do this is a fuller understanding—not just of our dreams, but also of deeper parts of ourselves. We can, however, begin to develop that fuller understanding by going on a journey inward and downward. Inch by inch, we'll lower ourselves inside and begin to view our inner terrain—and all the riches lying there waiting for us.

In this book, we'll explore your world of dreams as well as your world of sleep and learn how to decode the messages that your dreams may be trying to give you. In chapter 1, we'll learn about the myriad ways that working with your dreams can enrich your life, as well as what really happens while you're sleeping. We'll then cover some common questions about sleep and dreams in chapter 2, along with the answers to those questions and some fascinating facts. Where do your dreams come from? We'll look at that and different types of dreams in chapter 3.

There are some dreams that are fairly common, both nightmares and non-scary ones, and we'll go over them and what they might mean in chapter 4. I'll then share some recommendations for interpreting your dreams and a step-by-step procedure for doing so in chapter 5. In chapter 6, we'll start diving into dreams, with some dream samples, listed by type, and the interpretations of those dreams. You'll then get to practice interpreting some dreams yourself in chapter 7. I'll share my interpretations at the end of that chapter so you can compare your interpretations to mine. Please note that the dream samples are included verbatim insofar as possible, so as to maintain the integrity of the dreamers' accounts of their dreams and to retain subtle nuances of meaning evoked by the dreamers' literal wording when they recounted their dreams.

You'll want to work with your dreams after you've interpreted them so that you can take full benefit of the information and insight you gained, and I'll share various ways that you can do so in chapter 8. Then in chapter 9, I'll share some additional recommendations with you on working with your dreams. In the appendices, you'll find some helpful material on other ways to work with your dreams and how to explore and know your unconscious self.

Your dreams can reveal a whole new world to you, one that can be hugely rewarding. As you learn how to understand your dreams, you'll also learn to appreciate the deeper parts of yourself and how beneficial they can be to you.

What if you slept
And what if
In your sleep
You dreamed
And what if
In your dream
You went to heaven
And there plucked a strange and beautiful flower
And what if
When you awoke
You had that flower in your hand
Ah, what then?
—SAMUEL TAYLOR COLERIDGE

part I

Basics about Sleep and Dreams

one

Why Dreamwork?

Dreams capture our attention and intrigue us. This is not a recent phenomenon, as there are records of dreams dating back at least four thousand years. Both the Greeks and the Romans valued dreams, believing they had prophetic powers.

Aside from curiosity, why should we care about our dreams? We gain health benefits from sleep, but is there any benefit we can derive from paying attention to our dreams and striving to understand them?

Yes, there most definitely is. And not just one benefit. There are many potential benefits we can reap from working with our dreams.

Insights for Your Life Path: Dreams can give you insights for your personal unfolding and growth in life. There frequently are times when we may not realize that something is bothering us. Yet our dreams may be trying to tell us that there is something we need to address and work on for our personal welfare, unfolding, or greater happiness.

Health: Our dreams can give us information about our health—about how to optimize it and about potential problems, sometimes when we're consciously unaware of having a problem. There have been documented instances of people dreaming of various health concerns that motivated them to go see their doctor, only to have the dreamed-of health concern confirmed. There is even one project, the Breast Cancer Dreams Research Project, conducted by a friend and colleague of mine, Larry Burk, MD, that is gathering information on these instances, which you can participate in. (See his blog at www.letmagichappen.com/blog.) So your dreams can give you beneficial information about your health. Good thing, right?

Spiritual Guidance and Facilitation: There are obviously spiritual aspects of our dreams. We may be given guidance, information, or insight in our dreams. Passed-on loved ones, both human and animal, may visit us while we're sleeping and may communicate with us. Guides may also show up in our dreams, in order to give us information and "guide" us. We may be given psychic or intuitive information in our dreams—a warning about a negative future event, for example. We may also visit spiritual realms and dimensions while we're sleeping or dreaming or be given spiritual insight and counsel—and may even be worked with by guides and other spiritual beings in ways that trigger, accelerate, or guide our spiritual unfolding.

Problem-Solving: Another benefit of paying attention to our dreams has to do with problem-solving, as I mentioned earlier. Our unconscious works on problems for us in the sleep state (as well as while we're awake), and answers and solutions may be revealed to us in our dreams. You may have experienced this when you've gone to bed with a question on your mind and awakened in the morning with the answer.

Self-Awareness: A huge benefit of paying attention to and working with our dreams is that this can allow us to begin to glimpse and become aware of the deeper parts of ourselves—our unconscious.

Increasing research, much of which is covered in *Strangers to Ourselves: Discovering the Adaptive Unconscious* by Timothy D. Wilson, PhD, has revealed that we're not who we usually think we are. We typically identify ourselves with who we consciously feel we are—our conscious awareness and personality. However, our conscious awareness is just the tip of the iceberg. The largest part of who we are is all the stuff submerged below the water—our subconscious and unconscious, including our memories, fears, beliefs, mindset, etc. (See Appendix C: Knowing Your Whole Self—Befriending Your Unconscious.)

All that subterranean stuff—what we call our "personal stuff," meaning our wants, fears, needs, beliefs, mindset, etc.—guides our behavior and motivates us. It drives our behavior so much that we truly are not in full understanding or control of ourselves or our lives most of the time. It is only by diving into and exploring the deeper realms of ourselves that we not only learn more about ourselves and who we really are, but also become clearer in ourselves and freer of self-hindering obstacles. This is how we can place ourselves in the driver's seat of our lives and become masters of our own ship.

So there are many benefits to be gained from working with your dreams. It can be illuminating and inspiring and empowering!

Before we get into actually working with your dreams to enrich your life, let's talk about sleep. On the surface of it, there may not seem to be much to say, because we know that it's while we're sleeping that we dream. Seems simple enough, right? However, having a deeper understanding of sleep will truly help you work more effectively with your dreams.

Benefits of Sleep

Did you know that adequate sleep is crucial for dreaming? If you're sleep-deprived, you may not remember your dreams. It's important to take note of this, because unfortunately we live in a sleep-deprived society and many people try to get by on less sleep.

This is not the only reason why you'll want to get enough sleep, however, because adequate sleep benefits us in other critical ways, over and above remembering our dreams.

Sleep seems to have fallen somewhat out of favor in our modern, jam-packed lives. We may not value sleep, but adequate sleep is vital for our optimum functioning and health. We're learning more and more that sleep is crucial for certain health-related functions and brain maintenance. One thing that happens while we're sleeping is a consolidation of memories and recent events and experiences, similar to sorting through and filing away recent events and experiences. While we're sleeping, recent experiences are moved to more permanent storage in our brains. This includes learning new material—meaning that adequate sleep is vital to learning.

Tissue repair also occurs while we're sleeping, as does a sort of brain maintenance called "synaptic homeostasis" that primes the brain for new learning. A newer research finding from October 2013 that was reported on extensively revealed that a sort of brain cleaning occurs while we're sleeping (and not while we're awake), similar to the garbage being carted away, through a waste removal system that clears toxins (Mantel, 2013). It's been postulated that this brain cleaning may help to prevent Alzheimer's.

A large body of research has been conducted since the early 2000s yielding findings indicating that adequate sleep is vital for our health. Chronically getting inadequate sleep has been shown to add to and/or cause the following health conditions: obesity (because of two newly discovered hormones that regulate appetite); diabetes; cardiovascular disease, including higher cholesterol, heart disease, increased blood pressure, and an increased risk of stroke; a weakened immune system; emotionality; unethical behavior, including rudeness, inappropriate behavior, and dishonesty; depression; a greater difficulty in accurately reading others' faces and a heightened tendency to read threats where none exists; an increased risk of developing Alzheimer's; impaired judgment and becoming more prone to accidents; an increased risk of a shortened life span; a negative impact on brain development during adolescence; and a permanent loss of brain cells. Lack of sleep can also contribute to or worsen ADHD and be a risk factor for aggressive breast cancers.

So getting enough sleep is critical for your health and for learning. My own research has led me to conclude that adequate sleep is crucial for problem-solving as well.

Sleep really is your friend. If you want to be able to explore and understand your dreams, allow yourself to get enough sleep.

What Happens When You Sleep

You do it nightly, sometimes without even planning to. And yet your nighttime self may be as much of a stranger to you as an extraterrestrial visitor.

What happens when you sleep? Most of us are only familiar with our sleeping self through our dreams. Our conscious self seems to vanish, just go away, and then we reemerge in the morning as our "normal" self. Sleeps seems to be a black pit we know nothing about, aside from those vestiges of our dreams, which taunt us and haunt us.

Fortunately, research has been revealing more and more about what happens when we seemingly vanish at night. As a result of this illuminating work, increasing amounts of light are being shed on our slumbering "dark pit." Knowing what happens when you sleep will help you to decode and understand your dreams.

Levels of the Mind

A lot of changes take place within us when we fall asleep. The first change, of course, involves our consciousness. We descend into a deeper level of our mind, one that we may not be well acquainted with, but that is quite active while our conscious mind is sleeping and seemingly gone.

Understanding this process requires learning more about the various levels of our minds. Scientists have amassed more information about these levels through the study of brain waves, which are the measurable output of the brain's electrical impulses. So let's learn about them.

There are four primary types of brain waves, which are, from the fastest to the slowest, the following: beta, alpha, theta, and delta. There are qualities of consciousness associated with each.

Beta (13–30 Hertz)

Beta brain waves are associated with fast mental activity, active external attention, logical thinking, a sharp and focused mind, alertness, analytical problem-solving, and increased blood flow/metabolism, and are also present with fear, anger, anxiety, and worry (i.e., stress).

Alpha (8–12 Hertz)

Alpha brain waves occur while we're awake but not actively processing information and are associated with calmness and a feeling of ease, daydreaming, creative visualization, introspection, and creativity. They're the bridge between the conscious mind and the unconscious mind and help to allow us to peer below the surface of our consciousness. Alpha brain waves are also important for learning information, and they aid mental coordination and resourcefulness. We need to have enough of them going on in conjunction with other brain waves for optimal processing.

Theta (4–8 Hertz)

Theta brain waves are equated with the subconscious, which is a repository of memories, sensations, and emotions. These waves are slower and are associated with meditation, a heightened receptivity, inspiration, recall, hallucinations, and intuition. Theta brain waves predominate in the lighter levels of sleep and dreaming sleep (REM—rapid eye movement), although dreams can also occur in delta. Theta waves play a key role in coordinating different areas of the brain via gamma waves.

Delta (5–3 Hertz)

Delta brain waves occur in the deepest levels of sleep and represent the unconscious. They're associated with empathy and thin boundaries and deep trance states, and they represent a sort of radar that seeks out and receives information instinctually and orients us in time and space.

In addition to the previous four main types of brain waves, researchers have identified a fifth type relatively recently: gamma brain waves.

Gamma (30+ Hertz)

Gamma brain waves are associated with integrated thoughts, high-level information processing and perception, higher levels of insight, and states of self-awareness. These waves can induce the release of beta endorphins. In concert with theta waves, gamma brain waves help to transmit information among different brain regions.

Our Sleep Cycles

When we fall asleep, we descend from our waking states of consciousness—beta or alpha—down to theta and delta. Throughout the night, we cycle back and forth from the lighter levels of sleep (theta) down to deeper levels (delta), and then back again—up and down, over and over again. However, during the first part of our sleep cycle, we spend more time in the deeper levels of sleep. (In fact, scientists have further divided sleep into four stages, with stage 1 being the lightest and stage 4 the deepest.)

Whereas the thinking used to be that dreams occurred only during the lighter levels of sleep, it's now known that REM (rapid eye movement) sleep, the marker for dreams occurring, can happen during all stages of sleep, as can dreams with or without REM. (Rapid eye movement occurs while we're dreaming as our eyes seemingly track what we're seeing and experiencing during our dreams.) The dreams we tend to remember, however, occur more often during the lighter levels of sleep.

Interestingly, dreams can last for a wide range of time, anywhere from four minutes to seventy-two minutes.

The Physical Process of Sleep

In addition to the changes in our brain waves and consciousness, additional things shift when we go to sleep, including our brain and body chemicals. The one that many people are aware of is melatonin. We start to produce more of it in the evening as light from the sun fades, because it helps to induce sleep. Recent research, which was reported in a groundbreaking article in *Prevention* (Guthrie, 2005), indicates that melatonin may also kill cancer cells. In fact, it's important to turn off any source of light while we're sleeping, as a link has been found between exposure to light at night during the sleep cycle and a higher incidence of cancer.

Two additional changes help to create significant hallmarks of sleep. In one, neurons are turned off in our spinal cord, which helps to induce a paralysis in our bodies. Because of this, we tend not to physically act out our dreams. Interestingly, research has shown that there is a malfunction in this bodily mechanism in those who chronically sleepwalk. (See Schenck, 2008, and Rock, 2004.)

At the same time, two brain chemicals that circulate while we're awake, norepinephrine and serotonin, are turned off, and another neurotransmitter, acetylcholine, is produced. Acetylcholine triggers and excites the emotional, visual, and motor parts of our brain, which helps to explain why some dreams are arousing ones. Our limbic system, which has to do with emotions, is also fully activated while we're sleeping, resulting in our emotions being enhanced while we're dreaming.

In addition, the cerebral cortex in the brain is also tamped down. This is the part of the brain associated with higher reasoning and thinking, which allows us to focus, make logical connections, and compare experiences with reality. This is why dreams usually don't feel logical or unfold in a linear, logical fashion.

———

You now see how richly beneficial understanding and working with your dreams can be. You should also have a better grasp of what happens when you're sleeping and how different your sleeping mind is from your waking one. This knowledge can definitely be applied to your dreamwork. And, in order to work with your dreams, you'll want to record them. (We'll discuss this in more detail in the next chapter and in chapter 5.)

Next we'll look at some common questions about sleep and dreams, to give you a better grasp of your sleeping mind.

two

Common Questions and Facts about Sleep and Dreams

I've been asked many questions about sleep and dreams over the years whenever I've spoken, been interviewed, or taught classes about them, and I'm including several of them here along with their answers. The answers come from my own work and observations over the years, as well as from sleep and dream research over the past four decades. Becoming familiar with the answers to these questions should aid you in learning how to interpret and understand your dreams.

Common Questions about Dreams

Does everyone dream?

This is the single most commonly asked question I've encountered about dreams. Time after time when I've spoken about dreams, someone invariably says, "I don't dream."

The truth, however, is that almost everyone dreams, unless they have a brain abnormality or damage or are taking a medication that interferes with dreaming. (See Rock, 2004, and Cartwright, 2010.) Dreaming is a natural function of our brain while we're sleeping, so it's something quite natural and practically universal. Thus, in all likelihood, you *are* having dreams, whether you remember them or not.

Why don't I remember my dreams?

Early research on dreams (some of which was reported in *Dream Power* by Dr. Ann Faraday) showed that we tend to remember our dreams only when our level of consciousness shifts while we're dreaming. For example, we may hear a noise or we may need to shift our sleeping position.

If you're sleeping too soundly, you may not remember your dreams. If you're sleep-deprived and not getting enough sleep on a regular basis, you may be sleeping so soundly that very little could disturb your sleep, and thus you wouldn't be able to glimpse the lingering traces of a dream. In other words, you may be sleeping so soundly that it's almost impossible for you to remember your dreams.

If you have no interest in dreams, you may not be motivated to remember them. So having an interest in dreams is another factor in whether you're remembering your dreams.

Research shows that most people recall only 1 percent of their dreams. However, those who are more creative and who have a good memory tend to remember more of their dreams (Rock, 2004), and I feel that people who are introspective also tend to remember their dreams more than those who aren't. Research conducted by Luigi De Gennaro in 2011 has shown that people with more low-frequency theta brain waves in their frontal lobe are more likely to remember their dreams. A recent study revealed that people who tend to remember their dreams have heightened blood flow in certain regions of the brain and are more aware of external stimuli (Kim, 2014).

Why do I forget my dreams so quickly?

If you feel that you tend to remember dreams when you wake up and then find yourself unable to remember them later on, you're not alone. According to Michael Thorpy and Jan Yager (*The Encyclopedia of Sleep and Sleep Disorders*, 1991), and as cited in "60 Eye-Opening Facts About Sleep" (Randomhistory.com), we usually forget 50 percent of a dream within five minutes of waking up, and 90 percent within ten minutes. Dreams are ephemeral occurrences of our sleeping minds—the product of our sleeping "thinking," when our eyes are closed and our attention is focused inward. When we wake up, our brain waves change to those of a more waking consciousness and we're bombarded by external stimuli through our open eyes and other senses. Dream recall has little chance of surviving for long once all those external stimuli begin to flood in and crowd out the memory of our ephemeral dreams.

Even though most of our dreams vanish from our minds pretty quickly after we wake up, there are times when a fragment of a dream suddenly pops into our mind later on. It's usually triggered by something we experience the following day or so after having the dream. It could be a situation similar to the one we dreamed about, or to a person in the dream, or even to an event we dreamed about. Suddenly, out of the blue—bam! A slight memory of something from a dream appears in our mind—a slight fragment—and then maddeningly often disappears again just as quickly.

In the best of circumstances, it's virtually impossible to remember an entire dream for any length of time after waking up without recording it and trying to capture a detailed written account of it. That said, some powerfully moving dreams may stay with us for days—or even months or years; however, they are definitely the exception.

Can I learn to remember my dreams?

If you typically don't remember your dreams or even have a conscious awareness of them, you should be able to train yourself to remember them.

The first place to start is to consciously think about why you want to remember your dreams. (Recalling the benefits of dreams can be one thing that could motivate you.) Then remind yourself regularly that dreams can be beneficial and that you indeed want to remember yours.

Before you go to sleep, tell yourself, "I want to remember my dreams." Tell yourself this several times before going to sleep. You'll need to really *want* to remember them. Just saying the phrase won't necessarily work, as your unconscious knows whether you really want to or not and will disregard your statement if you don't care enough about this.

Allow yourself to wake up slowly and savor what was going through your mind before you woke up. If you have to wake up to an alarm clock, make sure the sound it makes isn't jarring.

Read about dreams and talk to other people about them. This will reinforce your new interest and remind your brain of it.

Over time, if you do these things regularly, you should find yourself remembering more of your dreams.

Why would I want to record my dreams?

Dreams can also offer us great insight for our personal and spiritual unfolding and growth in life. However, even with the best dream interpretation, the meanings and relevance of some dreams to our lives may take some time to be evident. So you'll want to have a written record of them.

By recording your dreams in a journal and reviewing them from time to time, things may leap out at you or make sense that hadn't at the time when you had the dream.

In a similar fashion, especially for dreams about your personal unfolding, reviewing your dreams from time to time can allow you to gauge how far you've come and grown. This can be quite rewarding and encouraging.

Dreams can be a hugely useful tool in your life, and recording them increases the potential of their usefulness to you.

What is the best way to record my dreams?

Try to record your dreams in as gentle and unobtrusive a way as possible. You can keep either a notebook and pen or a handheld digital recorder by your bed. Bear in mind, though, the critical importance of adequate sleep to your health, and try not to wake up too much to record your dreams or turn on the light to record them. Keeping a digital recorder right by your bed could enable you to quickly record your important dreams and then slip back to sleep.

Allow yourself to try these methods and see which you like more. Start keeping a dream journal now as you read this book and you'll have some dreams to interpret once we focus on how to do that. (You'll find more information on keeping a dream journal in chapter 5.)

Should I record every dream I have?

As you'll see in the next chapter, there are different types of dreams, and not every dream is significant. I personally recommend recording only significant dreams. If you try to record every dream you have, then you may be disturbing your sleep too much, too often, and unnecessarily.

How do I know whether a dream was significant?

We usually have a natural sense that a dream was significant in some way, even if we don't know why. We may have trouble putting the dream out of our mind, or it may continue to echo or reverberate in our mind over the next day or so.

Dreams that elicit strong emotions, such as bad dreams and nightmares, may also be significant.

There's no hard-and-fast rule of thumb or yardstick whereby we can determine or measure the significance of a dream. It truly is a judgment call, but, again, we usually have a sense as to whether a dream was significant or not if we find we can't put it out of our mind or it made a strong impact on us emotionally.

What are recurring dreams?

Recurring dreams are dreams that you have over and over again, whether in a short period of time, such as weeks or months, or over longer periods of time, such as years. Recurring dreams will often shift and evolve, or even develop more, over time.

Recurring dreams are frequently trying to give us a message. This could be about a personal issue in our lives, about a future event, or even about something from a past life that may have relevance for our present one. I have known people who have had the same recurring dreams since childhood and others for whom the recurring dreams lasted only for weeks.

If a recurring dream is giving us some sort of message about a future event, the dream will usually stop happening after the event occurs. If a recurring dream is about a personal issue, whether one in the present lifetime or one from a past life, the dream will often continue to happen and even evolve until the issue is worked on or has dissipated or been resolved.

Somewhat related to recurring dreams are serial dreams, which are dreams you have in a series that have somewhat different content but are related to each other.

How much do we dream each night?

We actually dream quite frequently when we sleep. We tend to dream throughout our sleep, but tend to have longer dreams later in the sleep cycle, often with more people and events from our past. We also tend to remember more of our dreams in the lighter levels of sleep. Dreams in the deeper levels of sleep tend to be more fragmentary and not remembered.

If we sleep later than usual, we have a greater tendency to have especially vivid and memorable dreams, according to research conducted by John Antrobus of the City University of New York (Rock, 2004).

We usually have several dreams each night, whether we remember all of them or not.

Why are some dreams so bizarre?

It's important to realize that there are different sources of dreams, which we'll cover in the next chapter. Many, if not most, stem from our unconscious, and our unconscious has a very different vocabulary from our conscious mind. In addition, while we're sleeping, our cortex, the seat of logic and higher reasoning, is "turned off" or inactive, as is the language center of our brain, while the part of the brain that processes connotations and associations is still on. While we're awake, our conscious mind relies on the left hemisphere and language center in the brain to name and categorize things. This is part of what is shut off while we sleep, so our unconscious uses other means to convey things, such as situations, connotations, events, feelings, analogies, pictorial representations, etc.

It's important to remember that it is the unconscious that is primarily operative while we're sleeping, and it tends to operate by stream of consciousness and association. Interestingly, our brain itself is also associative. However, our unconscious takes this to a new level.

The way the unconscious mind works while we're sleeping can be somewhat paradoxical, because it can be quite literal at times, while also making allusions and associations, and it loves puns and plays on words. We'll get into this in more detail when we go over how to interpret and understand dreams later in the book.

So our unconscious mind has its own vocabulary and language, which tends to seem quite foreign to our conscious mind. It's not what we're used to in our waking life, but we can learn how to understand its "speech" and its "language" when it speaks to us in our dreams. Once we learn the language of our unconscious, we will frequently find ourselves amazed by how much our unconscious has to say to us, how much meaningful and helpful information it has to convey to us, and how much sense it makes.

Why do I remember more bad dreams than good ones?

Our dreams are ephemeral and quickly forgotten, like smoke dissipating before our eyes—and you'll recall that we tend to remember our dreams only when our level of consciousness shifts during them. So we may sleep through many of our dreams and not remember them, especially if their emotional content is fairly neutral.

If we have a bad dream, however, the unpleasant nature of it and the negative emotions it generates can trigger our memory of it. Something negative will often get our attention more than something neutral will, and a negative or scary dream can startle us or shift our sleep level, causing us to remember it.

If a dream is really pleasant and thus triggers a strong positive feeling, that could also trigger our attention, stimulating a slight awakening and thus a memory of the dream. Unfortunately, those bad dreams will often get our attention more than the pleasant ones, causing us to remember more of them than the good ones.

Why do I have nightmares?

It's important to differentiate between bad dreams and nightmares. A nightmare is a bad dream that's so negatively arousing that it wakes us up. If a bad dream doesn't wake you up, it's considered to be a bad dream and not a nightmare.

While nightmares can be triggered by causes other than emotions, such as illness or fever, withdrawal from drugs, some prescription medications (notably antidepressants and blood pressure drugs), or sleep disorders, they are often triggered by negative emotions, such as fear, anxiety, worry, stress, guilt, confusion, sadness, disgust, dislike, and even hatred. If there's an issue we're currently dealing with in our life—financial worries, for example—the concern or fear will often intrude into our dream state. For example, if we're struggling financially and having difficulty paying our bills, we might not just have trouble getting to sleep or find ourselves waking up in the middle of the night, we might also have a nightmare about being out on the street or alone in the world and feeling completely vulnerable.

Likewise, unresolved issues from the past can also trigger nightmares. If we experienced abuse as a child, whether physical or emotional, and we haven't resolved those issues through therapy or other therapeutic means, we may have nightmares triggered by the unresolved issues.

I had a client who had chronic nightmares. When he shared them with me, I suspected childhood abuse and asked him if that was the case, which he confirmed. As it turned out, he had never undergone therapy for the abuse, and his nightmares were expressing this ongoing inner conflict. Even though he consciously felt that the abuse was no problem and was behind him, his nightmares were evidence of him being haunted by the childhood abuse that had never been healed or resolved. He may have consciously felt that the abuse was behind him, but the issues it created were still quite active in his unconscious.

So why would issues we haven't addressed or resolved create nightmares?

Nightmares are usually our unconscious mind's way of drawing our attention to issues we have that are affecting our mind and preventing it from being whole. We may consciously feel that everything is okay, whereas the reality may be that those old unhealed issues are still roiling around in our unconscious and they represent a disharmony within our consciousness. On some level, they are stressing us. Our unconscious is quite aware of their presence and effects on our psyche and will often render them to our conscious awareness in the form of a nightmare. This is not a bad thing. Rather, it's quite helpful and can let us know that something is bothering us on a deep level, even if we're not consciously aware of it. Once we know that, we can choose to work on healing the issue in some way.

I feel that our unconscious is always trying to bring us into balance. Things that are out of balance—worry, stress, unresolved issues, etc.—represent things in us that are out of sync; and when our psyche is not in balance, those issues will often be expressed through dream content, either to draw our attention to what needs to be looked at or as a means of unconsciously working through some of it. So our unconscious mind puts these disharmonies into dreams to bring our attention to them. It's as if it's trying to tell us, "Hey, there's something out of balance that you need to deal with." It's then up to us to do something about it, to heal it and brings ourselves to wholeness and inner balance, which is, after all, better for our overall health and well-being.

Some people feel that nightmares can also serve as a type of relief valve, releasing some of the negative emotions for us so that they don't build up. That may indeed be true at times, although I tend to look at nightmares as giving us a signal steering us to what needs to be dealt with.

A nightmare can also be precognitive and could be giving us information about a future negative event. This type of nightmare may not be expressing a fear, but it can be scary nonetheless. Although we can't necessarily avert a future negative event from happening, having a nightmare about it can help to prepare us for it in some way.

If we look at nightmares from this perspective, they can be quite useful tools, right? And our unconscious is really useful too when it performs this function for us, because it's just trying to bring us to balance and wholeness.

Can a dream have more than one meaning?

Yes, a dream can certainly have more than one meaning that's valid for the dreamer, just as any one symbol in a dream can have more than one meaning that's valid for the dreamer. This speaks to the beautiful complexity of dreams.

You'll note that I wrote "valid for the dreamer." I wrote that for a reason.

Any one dream can have numerous possible meanings. In this way, dream interpretation can be similar to explication of literature, in which we analyze literature for all its potential meanings, including via symbolism. However, you'll want to find the meaning or meanings of a dream that are valid for the person who had the dream, and not every possible meaning. When I've taught classes on dreams and opened up the session for attendees to practice interpreting other people's dreams, I have frequently seen some people try to put their spin on someone else's dream. It's always important to remember that if you're interpreting someone else's dream, *it's that person's dream, not yours*. As a result, you'll want to help that person find the meanings of the dream that are valid for that individual. We gain the most insight from our dreams when we learn what their meanings are specifically for us.

I have marveled over the years at how many meanings one dream can have, so remember this when interpreting a dream. You'll want to capture the full richness of a dream by finding all its valid meanings for the person who had the dream.

Why do we dream of someone from our distant past?

Some people are taken aback when they have a dream with someone appearing in it whom they haven't thought of in many years. This usually isn't a random occurrence; on the contrary, there is often a reason why this happens.

Much of the research conducted in the past few years has revealed that one of the primary things that happens while we're sleeping or dreaming is the reinforcement of learning. In other words, new things that we learned or were exposed to during the day are reinforced in our memory (laid down more permanently in our brains) while we're sleeping. You'll recall that we touched upon this earlier. Our brains take the events and new information we were exposed to during our waking hours and process it in order to file away what we need to retain more permanently in our brains and minds. Because the brain is associative, it will search through the new experiences and information for relevance and relationship to what we already know and have learned—in other words, what is already in our memory bank.

So, for example, if we encounter someone who either unconsciously reminds us of or is similar in some way to someone from our past, we may have a dream in which that person from our past plays a prominent role. I've spoken to a few female clients who were in a relatively new relationship and who had a dream of a former boyfriend or love interest because their new love interest reminded them unconsciously on some level of that former love interest. This is far from uncommon.

Let's say you had a prior relationship with someone who was controlling. You may be in a new relationship or be interested in someone who behaves in a similar manner, even though you may not consciously realize it. Your unconscious, though, which knows you better and sees things more clearly than you do, has noted the similarity and produces a dream with the former love interest in it.

This type of dream can happen with all types of relationships, not just romantic ones. You could interview for a job and have a dream that night about a former teacher who seemed to persecute you or one who was a joy to study under.

If you have a dream in which someone from your past appears, look for what or who in your present life could be similar. Then try to determine the message of the dream.

Are all dreams the same type of thing— just dreaming about something?

No, not all dreams are just dreaming *about* something, and this also speaks to the beautiful complexity of dreaming. Some dreams are actual experiences. While you're sleeping, your consciousness can be off exploring other places geographically or even be in other time periods, whether from the past, including past lives, or the future. You can also astral-travel to other places.

Another type of dream that is an actual experience is a dream in which you are communicating with someone else. We'll discuss this when we explore the various types of dreams in the next chapter.

For now, suffice it to say that some dreams represent dreaming about something, while other dreams can be actual experiences.

Can you communicate with someone else while you're sleeping?

Yes, you can. You can communicate with friends and loved ones, both living and passed-on (including both humans and animals), as well as guides, angels, higher spiritual beings, and others. Our mouth may not work the same, or our ears, as when we're awake, but we can communicate through our larger mind, unconscious, and higher self, whether we would call this telepathy or not. Communication with others isn't restricted to occurring solely while we're awake.

Is there anything that goes on in the deepest levels of sleep other than dreams?

Many people say there is. Some feel that we are worked with by guides and other spiritual beings in the deepest levels of sleep. This can include us being taught and shown things, as well as being taken to other levels and dimensions, for our personal unfolding and enrichment. Many people also feel that they do healing work and help others while they're sleeping, and some have a memory of having done that.

Sometimes I wake up knowing the answer to something that was on my mind when I went to bed. Can I learn how to make that happen more often?

Yes, it is indeed true that you can wake up with an answer to something—and that you can learn how to work with this. This is called incubating a dream. It's not a foolproof technique, but your unconscious will work on problems that are important to you, including while you're sleeping.

It isn't too difficult to learn how to incubate a dream, and we'll discuss it at greater length in chapter 8. Just know for now that you'll need to really *want* to know the answer to something. This is because the emotional part of your brain, the amygdala, needs to be charged and involved, because it can affect motivation. Before going to sleep, just tell your-self—*with feeling*—that you really *want* to have a dream that will give you an answer about _____. (You fill in the blank with the specific problem or issue.)

You might have to do this a few times before you suc-ceed, but you should find success at some point.

Is it true that eating a spicy meal before you go to sleep will affect your dreams?

Yes, it could. Some foods can affect dream content or qual-ity of sleep, as can alcohol and some medications. If a food doesn't sit well in your stomach, meaning that it either upsets your stomach or you have trouble digesting it, that physical discomfort could intrude into your dreams and affect the content of them.

In addition, your sleep-wake cycle is affected by the light cycle as well as neurotransmitters in your brain, and some foods can affect these signals. Drinking coffee or tea with caf-feine can interfere with sleep, as can heavy smoking. Some foods, medications, and alcohol can affect the quality of sleep and the levels of sleep, thus affecting or interfering with dreaming and dream content.

I've had dreams about my health at times. Can a dream tell you about an illness you didn't know you had?

Yes, a dream can most definitely let you know that you have an illness that you were not consciously aware of. As

I shared before, there have been instances of people having a dream in which they had an illness—a woman dreaming of having breast cancer, for example, and then having the illness later confirmed by a doctor. (Dr. Robert L. Van de Castle cites some examples of this in his excellent book *Our Dreaming Mind*.) However, just because you dream that you have an illness doesn't mean that you really do have it. The dream could be stemming from a fear you have, or the illness could symbolize something else.

It's a judgment call as to what has triggered a dream about having an illness. The best thing to do is to determine whether the dream was truly trying to give you a message about a health condition, or if it might have been expressing a fear or something else.

For a dream that is indeed letting us know that we have an illness, we can be grateful for the dream. After all, it is cueing us in to something we may not have realized we had and that might not manifest with obvious symptoms for quite some time, and with some illnesses timely diagnoses and treatments can be critical. An early heads-up via a dream could be potentially lifesaving.

Can a scary movie affect my dreams?

Yes, it can. If you watched a TV show or movie that was arousing (triggering strong feelings in you of fear, anger, longing, etc.), your dreams may reflect the content of what you watched or express the feelings you had. This is especially true if you watched something arousing shortly before going to bed.

It's best to watch or read neutral things within two to three hours of going to bed. That way, your dreams won't be acting out the war movie you saw or scaring you from the horror film you watched.

Does everyone dream in the same way or style?

No, and this also speaks to the richness of dreams. We all tend to have our own individual style of dreaming. Some people may tend to have dreams that are fairly short, while others may have longer ones. (Remember that research has shown that dreams can last from four to seventy-two minutes.) Some people may dream of themselves as if they were watching themselves, while others may dream from their typical point of observation inside themselves. Some people may dream as the opposite sex (which could be past-life related). If a movie or even cartoon was important or affected a person, the individual may dream as a character from the movie or cartoon because of the character's traits that made an impression.

When I was in graduate school, my roommate, who was also interested in dreams, and I would discuss our dreams in the morning and interpret each other's dreams. My roommate tended to have long, involved, technicolor dreams, while my dreams tended to be shorter and in black and white or muted colors. I've interpreted many dreams over the years, and some have been fairly short and simple, while others have been longer and more complex.

Interestingly, your style of dreaming can shift over time. I tend to dream in more color now than I used to. So try not to compare your style of dreaming with anyone else's. There's no one "right" way to dream. The styles are highly individualistic.

Are children's dreams different from adults'?

Yes, they are. Very young children, usually under age five, tend to have dreams without much of a storyline, and they can be prone to have more nightmares than the average adult. Children also tend to have animals appear prominently in their dreams more often than adults do.

Surprisingly, children also have aggressive dreams about twice as much as adults. Some theorize that this is because children are in the process of developing better impulse control. During the teen years, dreams tend to become more like those of adults.

Do women and men dream differently?

Yes, research has indicated that the genders do tend to have different dream content. Men tend to dream more about other men, while women give equal time in their dreams to both genders. Women also tend to remember their dreams more than men and have more nightmares than men, while men tend to dream more about sex. (No surprise there!)

In addition, what may also not come as a surprise is that men tend to dream more about aggressive encounters with other men, while women tend to dream about familiar places and people. In addition, men's nightmares tend to be more about natural disasters and war or physical aggression, while women's tend to be more about interpersonal conflict. (See "New Study Analyzes Content of Nightmares and Bad Dreams" on MedicalXpress.com, 2014.)

Do animals dream?

We don't have a definitive answer to that question yet. We do know that animals exhibit REM sleep, which would seem to indicate dreaming, as it's a marker in humans for dreaming, but researchers feel that the jury is still out on this question. Others among us, myself included, feel that animals do dream, especially when we see some of them, such as dogs, twitching and barking with their paws moving.

Do blind people dream?

Yes, blind people do dream. We don't know whether they're seeing in their dreams, but they do indeed dream. We may tend to feel that sight is required for dreaming and that our dreams are primarily visual experiences, but this is not necessarily true. Other senses can be part of the dreaming experience, such as smell, taste, touch, and hearing.

Research such as that reported in "The Dreams of Blind Men and Women" (Hurovitz, Dunn, Domhoff, and Fiss, 1999) has shown that some people who are blind may be seeing in some of their dreams, depending upon whether they ever had sight and the age at which they became sightless. Those born blind and those who lost their sight at a very young age tend to have visual dreams the least.

Whether visual imagery is present in their dreams or not, those who are blind do indeed dream.

If you dream that you die or are killed, do you really die?

Many people have dreams in which they are fatally injured or even murdered, but they don't really die. This is a scary scenario in a dream, but it shouldn't be lethal unless it triggers a fatal heart attack out of fear.

Can I influence my dreams?

Yes, you can. You may already be unconsciously influencing your dreams through your habits, such as not getting enough sleep, what you eat or drink, what you watch on TV, the medications you take, etc. Quitting smoking cold turkey, as opposed to gradually cutting down, can result in more vivid dreams. You may not be intending to influence dreams in that way, but your behavior may indeed be having an effect on them.

You can also decide to influence a dream while you are having it. This is called "lucid dreaming," and increasing numbers of people are practicing it. Technically it's called this because you become lucid in the dream and aware that you are dreaming. We'll be discussing lucid dreaming in appendix B.

Does it matter if you dream in color or black and white? Is there any meaning to dreaming in one or the other?

Twelve percent of people dream in black and white as opposed to color. This number was even higher before the invention of color TV and movies, earlier in the twentieth century. However, if one goes back even further in time, research thus far indicates that people still were largely dreaming in color (Gonzalez, 2011). That said, there usually isn't any meaning or judgment if you tend to dream in one or the other. The exception would be if a segment of a dream was in black and white while the rest of the dream was in color, or vice versa. This could be relevant, and you would need to look at the whole dream to determine its meaning, if any.

Additional Helpful and Interesting Facts about Sleep and Dreams

Here is some information that could be helpful to you in understanding and working with your dreams.

- We can only dream of faces we've actually seen before.

- Going without sleep for ten days could be fatal.

- A reduction in dreaming lowers our ability to understand complex emotions in daily life. Some research shows that dreams help to regulate moods.

- Most dreams involve normal situations with familiar people. Bizarre, intense, or fantastical dreams are the exception.

- Positive emotions, such as joy, also appear in dreams, as do surprise, anger, anxiety, and sadness.

- We dream in the womb, before we are born—and this fact can elicit some intriguing possibilities.

- Violent dreams can be an early warning sign of later brain disorders, such as Parkinson's disease and dementia.

- The part of the brain that is considered to be critical for self-awareness is more active during dreaming.

- People in the United States have the highest amount of aggression in their dreams among modern, industrialized countries, although people in small tribal societies tend to have the greatest amount of physical aggression proportionally (Rock, 2004).

- It's rare to dream of reading, writing, or arithmetic.

- If humans are prevented from dreaming, they can develop various personality disorders and psychological problems.
- Dream recall is greater if you wake up during the dream.
- Not all dreams have hidden meaning. Some will be literal or straightforward.

Being aware of some of the answers to common questions about dreams and known facts about sleep and dreams can help you to understand your world of sleep and interpret and work with your dreams. Next we'll turn our attention to where dreams come from and the various types of dreams.

three

Sources and Types of Dreams

Have you ever wondered where your dreams come from? In working with dreams over the years, I have observed that there are various possible sources of dreams, in addition to different types of them. Most of us tend to think that all dreams come from our minds—from our unconscious. I have learned that this is not true. There are, in fact, additional possible sources of our dreams. There are also different types of dreams, and we'll learn about them in this chapter as well.

This is important information for us to have, because it does have bearing on interpreting and understanding our dreams.

Sources of Dreams

Our dreams can come from various possible sources, and some dreams can potentially come from more than one source.

The Unconscious

Our unconscious will be the source of many, if not most, of our dreams. You'll remember that one of the functions of sleep has to do with learning. It is while we're sleeping that we're consolidating and moving to more permanent storage the events experienced and things learned during the day or preceding day. This "file maintenance" often triggers dreams. Brain maintenance (synaptic homeostasis) also takes place during sleep, as you'll recall. The jury is still out on whether this brain maintenance also triggers dreams or not.

Additionally, you'll remember that your unconscious is usually trying to bring your mind into balance and seeks to bring to your conscious awareness any imbalances (from fears, wishes, outdated modes of being or thought, unrecognized possibilities, mental chores, old self-defeating or limiting issues, etc.). Your unconscious will frequently yield these insights up to you in the form of dreams.

Even dreams that are intuitive or psychic will likely stem from your unconscious at times, as the delta brain waves of your unconscious serve the purpose of acting as a sort of radar, sussing out the environment in order to pull in relevant or important information.

So your unconscious should be viewed as one of the main sources of your dreams.

Other People and Beings

Yes, other people and beings can be a source of your dreams. This includes living people, those who have passed on, spiritual beings (including guides, angels, etc.), and animals, both living and passed-on. Any of these can create some of your dreams.

Usually dreams that stem from others will be those in which communication takes place. However, it's also possible that some dream scenarios may be triggered by others (other people, spiritual beings, or animals) even if they don't include communication or messages. Other people, beings, or animals could be giving us a dream.

It's often while we're sleeping that passed-on loved ones, including animals, will be able to communicate with us or visit us. Many of us tend to tune out any awareness of the presence of passed-on loved ones while we're awake (although there are certainly people who are indeed consciously aware of them). We're in a more porous state of consciousness while we're sleeping, making us much more receptive to this type of communication and visitation.

The living can also be the source of some of our dreams. Many people communicate with friends and loved ones while sleeping and carry on two-way conversations. Have you ever had a dream in which you felt like you were talking to someone you knew? And did you then ask the other person the next day or soon afterward about the dream? Did the other person then confirm having had the same type of dream that same night? If so, then you were likely "talking" to each other in the dream—communicating telepathically during the sleep state.

People can communicate with each other in the dream state in a less direct way as well. When I was in graduate school, there were a few nights on which my roommate and I had the same dream, with the same elements in each of our dreams. That was stunning to me the first time it happened. This showed me that deep communication can happen in a way I found to be quite unexpected. There are dream groups in which the members try to have dreams for other members, but I'm not sure if members have identical dreams on the same nights.

There are terms that some people use to refer to this latter type of dream. Some call it "mutual dreaming," while others use the term "meeting dreams" or "meshing dreams." There are theories about virtual or alternate realities in which these shared dreams exist. To me, however, they may reveal the closeness and entwined energies of the two people who have these shared, similar dreams. One variation on this type of mutual dreaming is having a dream *for* someone else. For example, if a friend of yours has been ill, you could have a dream about your friend's illness that gives information about it that you could then share with your friend. This is not a shared dream as much as it is having a dream specifically *about* or *for* someone else.

The fact that dreams can derive from others, whether living or dead, human or animal, is one that many of us overlook. However, others can indeed be a source of some dreams.

Physical Conditions

As you'll recall, the condition of our bodies while we're sleeping can be the source of some of our dreams. This can include our bladders being full, our body's response to the ambient temperature being too low or too high, having a fever, or even experiencing uncomfortable conditions in our stomach.

You may have a dream, for example, in which you're trudging through deep snow in Siberia, shivering in the cold and looking for shelter. You then wake up and find that you are indeed cold because the temperature in your bedroom is chilly. Likewise, you may dream that you overdid physical exercise and the muscles in your calves are really sore. You wake up and discover that you have a cramp in your right leg.

Dreams that stem from conditions in your body aren't all mundane, however. You can also have dreams that are telling you about a health issue you didn't realize you had, as touched upon in the last chapter. Dreams like this stem from conditions in the body, but can be far from insignificant.

Whether a dream is mundane or significant in nature, keep in mind that your body can be the source of some of the dreams you have.

External Conditions

External conditions, including those in your bedroom, house, or outside, can also be the source of dreams. This can include conditions such as noise, weather, or even smoke or fire (certainly unpleasant to contemplate).

Think of warm nights when some people sleep with their windows open. Enter a cat or two outside that may be in heat or feisty enough to want to fight other cats—and perhaps a melee starts. There may be loud feline noises, screeching, and other disturbing sounds. You may find yourself dreaming about a cat, in which case the cat(s) outside would be the source of your dream. If the external noises get loud enough, you might be awakened by them. Before that happens, though, you might be dreaming about a cat or two.

We may feel that our dreams are somewhat "pure" events that spring from within us and are unaffected by anyone or anything else. This, however, is far from the truth. External conditions can not only intrude upon our dreams, but also cause some of them.

Higher Soul Awareness

Our higher soul awareness and even very high-level spiritual beings can also be the source of some of our dreams. This can include being told or taught something in a dream and can extend to being worked on in some way, usually having to do with spiritual matters.

As mentioned earlier, there are those who feel that spiritual teachings and deep work often take place in the deepest levels of sleep, although we may not always have a memory of these dream experiences. I feel that this is true for me. I have a sense at times that I've been worked with on a deep level, but I have no conscious memory of a dream or what transpired.

We can also receive communications and have dream content from our higher soul awareness and spiritual beings that we remember. It's wonderful that we have this type of spiritual resource while we're here on Earth and that we can be worked with in this manner, all to benefit our personal and spiritual unfolding and growth. This is a tantalizing thought, and it would be wonderful to have a more conscious awareness or memory of these experiences.

Types of Dreams

Now let's look at the various possible types of dreams. There are several different types of dreams, and some can stem from more than one possible source.

Sorting Information, Filing It Away, and Learning from It

You'll remember that one of the aspects of our sleep and dreams has to do with learning—taking the new experiences and information of the day and moving it from temporary memory to more permanent storage in the brain. It's a sort of filing activity.

As a result, one type of dream is purely that of sorting through information from the day and filing it away. Dreams like this may or may not be significant. The significant ones may trigger connections or correlations to people or experiences from our past, especially if the memory from our past was significant or emotionally charged in any way. Because the brain is associative, our memory banks will be searched during the process of sorting and filing for correlation when filing away events from the day. If a present event or person triggers or is associated with one from our past, we may find ourselves dreaming of the past situation or person.

Depending upon the importance of the past event or person, a dream containing that information could be a significant one for us. You'll recall the example given earlier in chapter 2 about encountering someone in your life who unconsciously reminds you of someone from your past who was controlling. This is significant information for us to have in order to avoid repeating any mistakes from our past with potentially similar ones in our present, and having dreams like this represents another way in which our unconscious is trying to assist us.

Dreams of this type usually stem from our unconscious and may or may not be significant. It's up to us to determine whether they are or not.

Expression of Bodily Conditions

Some dreams may solely be expressing conditions in our bodies, as discussed earlier, and are obviously stemming from the body. These can include not only mundane dreams, such as "bathroom dreams," dreams reflecting the ambient temperature, and so on, but also dreams that express health conditions. Whereas a bathroom dream may not be a significant one, a dream expressing a health condition could be a very important one and one that we would want to pay attention to.

You could have a dream expressing a health condition in your body—*and* it's also possible to have a dream about a health condition that someone else has. This will usually happen when the dreamer is close to the person dreamed about, but could also happen if the person dreamed about is important to the dreamer, whether they know each other directly or not. So this type of dream will include dreams that are expressing bodily conditions, even if it's not a physical condition in your own body.

Message Dreams

In dreams of this type, you're being given a message. The message could come from another person (whether living or passed-on), a guide or other spiritual being, or an animal.

Dreams in which you receive a message are often significant ones, depending upon the content of the message and the source of it. Obviously, if the communication is with a passed-on loved one, it will usually be considered to be significant. If it accomplishes nothing else, it lets us know that our loved one is still "alive," even if just in consciousness.

Communication Dreams, Including Visitation

This type of dream may at first glance look like it's the same as a message dream. However, it's not. If you think about it, receiving a message is one-way communication. Communication dreams are two-way communications, in which there is a two-way "conversation."

As mentioned earlier, there are times when we are actually communicating with someone else in a dream, whether someone we know who's alive, a passed-on loved one, a guide or other spiritual being, or an animal, whether living or passed-on. It's like having a conversation with someone else, even if it's a telepathic one.

Expressing Fears and Desires

This type of dream includes bad dreams and nightmares, which are often expressing our inner fears or other unpleasant feelings, whether we're consciously aware of those feelings or not. It would also include some pleasant dreams, those in which desires are being expressed. One might consider a flying dream to be an example of a dream expressing a wish, given the feeling of freedom, pleasure, and liberation that we usually have with such dreams—unless the flying dream is an actual experience rather than simply the expression of a wish.

Dreams of this type could stem from our unconscious or even our higher soul awareness or a guide, if we're being asked, for example, to look at and heal a fear or to consider working with something we love.

Dreams that express our desires and wishes may also be significant, especially if they reveal to us a desire that we were not consciously aware of.

Creative Inspiration and Problem-Solving

This type is one example of the beauty of dreams. Some dreams give us ideas and some can help us to solve problems. To me, this shows one specific way in which our dreams can benefit us and how our unconscious can as well.

Have you ever gone to sleep with a problem on your mind and then awakened in the morning knowing the answer? This experience happens to many people, and the inspiration can pertain to mundane issues, artistic creations, scientific information, and other forms of problem-solving.

Several well-known people have experienced this. The following are some examples of famous people who got ideas or solved problems in their sleep:

- Richard Wagner received the inspiration for his opera *Tristan and Isolde* from a dream.
- The last movement of Handel's *Messiah* was inspired by a dream.
- Steve Allen wrote the popular song "This Could Be the Start of Something Big" based upon a dream he had.
- Mary Shelley received the inspiration for *Frankenstein* in a dream. She was staying with friends,

including Percy Bysshe Shelley (her future husband), Lord Byron, and others. They challenged each other to see who could write the best horror story. Weeks later, she dreamt about a scientist who created life and then wrote her well-known book.

- Dmitri Mendeleev received information on his version of the periodic table of elements in a dream.

- The scientist Kekulé was working on determining the structure of the benzene molecule. Sitting in a chair in front of the fireplace, he dozed and dreamed of atoms that turned into long rows and then turned into snakes biting each other's tails and whirling in a circle. He woke up realizing that this was the structure of the molecule.

- Jack Nicklaus went through a period of time in which his golf game was off. One night he dreamed about what was wrong with his swing and how to correct it. He applied what he had been shown in his dream and his game improved again.

- Elias Howe, when designing the sewing machine, was stumped about where the thread would go through the needle. He received a solution to this problem in a dream in which there were savages with spears that had eye-shaped holes near the pointed tips of the spears. He woke up knowing where to situate the hole on the needle.

As you can see, getting ideas or solving problems through your dreams can be a huge benefit to you in your life.

Dreams like these can stem from a variety of sources, including our unconscious, our higher soul awareness, and even a guide or passed-on loved one.

We can learn how to groom our minds to increase the likelihood of having a dream that solves a problem or gives us an idea. This is called "dream incubation," which we touched upon briefly in chapter 2. We'll be discussing it in more detail in chapter 8.

Expressing Personal Issues and Personal Process, and Working Issues Out

We touched upon this earlier, when I shared that in some dreams our unconscious is seeking to bring us to balance and helps us work on old unresolved, self-defeating personal issues. This type of dream is far from uncommon. I'll share with you a dream that I feel illustrates this type of dream perfectly.

I had a client call me about a dream that really perplexed him. He was a medical student at Duke. In his dream, he was on a really long train ride, dressed up as a vampire. Even though he was stumped by his dream, to me the meaning was really clear.

I asked him, "You didn't really want to be a doctor, did you?" He shared that he didn't, but that his parents wanted him to be one. How did I know this from the dream?

In his dream, it was taking a long time to get to his destination. Just consider medical school, residency, internship—it takes years to become a physician. In addition, he was dressed in a costume, indicating that he felt that he wasn't himself. His being a vampire also indicated that he felt like he was sucking others' blood.

So you see that all the elements were there in his dream to give that interpretation, although they were cloaked in symbols.

After I shared this with him, he said that he had to be a doctor simply because that was what his parents wanted him to be. He said that he wanted to be a geologist, but that he needed to comply with his parents' wishes. I replied that it was his life to live and that I hoped he would focus on what he wanted as opposed to living his life according to others' wishes.

This is an excellent example of a dream that expresses personal issues. In his conscious mind, my client felt that he had to be a doctor and was resigned to it. However, his unconscious was screaming out, "I'm not comfortable! This isn't me!" And his unconscious expressed his inner conflict via the dream. I've often wondered whether he stayed in medical school and became a doctor after all.

This type of dream gives us information from deep within ourselves and often stems from our unconscious, our higher soul awareness, and/or a guide. If there's an unresolved issue from our past that's blocking us or holding us back, we may have a dream about it. If there's a situation in our lives at present that's problematic, we may have this type of dream about it as well. This type of dream can also express wishes that spring from deep within us and that we may not be consciously aware of. Having this type of dream can also be a way of working through personal issues.

Because this type of dream deals with our unconscious seeking to bring us to balance and wholeness, dreams of this type are often significant ones that we will want to pay attention to, decode, follow up on, and work with in some way.

Healing Dreams

Healing dreams are similar to dreams that are expressing personal issues and personal process, and working issues out, except that healing dreams actually produce a type of healing or show us what needs to be healed or how to heal something. Another way to look at these two types would be that dreams that are expressing personal issues are often expressing the issue or problem area (such as expressing fears, as in nightmares), whereas healing dreams will trigger a healing or will point to how we can bring one about. The healing could relate to a physical condition or an emotional issue.

For example, you may find yourself dreaming that you're in a forest walking around. Suddenly you see a shaft of light shining on one particular plant. You walk over to the plant to get a closer look at it and then realize that it's almost identical to a photo you've seen before. You wake up with the word "comfrey" in your mind. You've had a skin problem and decide to do some online research and discover that comfrey can be made into a poultice or salve that is said to be excellent for healing different skin problems. A dream like this is healing because it's given you a remedy for a health condition.

You can also have a dream that heals an issue in your life, perhaps an issue from your childhood or one in the present, including emotional issues. Some people have had dreams that actually helped them heal emotionally or psychologically. We can try to incubate healing dreams, although we tend to have healing dreams when the time is right for the healing to take place.

Healing dreams, whether spontaneous or incubated, are wonderful and are obviously quite helpful, and will usually come from our unconscious, our higher soul awareness, and/or a guide.

Psychic Dreams, Including Precognition, Clairvoyance, etc.

Our dreams can indeed have psychic elements in them, including precognition, in which we're shown a future event; clairvoyance, in which we may glimpse something we would have no way of seeing; and other types of intuitive forms. People often think of psychic dreams when they think of dreams that are significant.

You may have a clairvoyant dream, for example, in which you see your grandmother making your favorite dessert and then find out when speaking to her the next day that she was doing just that at the exact time you had the dream. Psychic dreams can come from our unconscious, a guide, or our higher soul awareness.

Dreams that are psychic are much more common than we realize, especially those that are precognitive. With precognitive dreams, we often have an aha moment when the dreamed-of event happens, unless we have forgotten about the dream by that time.

Not everyone is comfortable having psychic dreams, especially if they are precognitive ones about negative events. One person in my dream group shared the following:

This is somewhat odd, but when I was a child of about nine years of age, I would dream of, for example, a plane crash, and to my horror, on the evening news would come the report of a major crash with the associated loss of life. I was confused; I did not know if I was predicting these events or, worse yet, causing them. So I began to suppress my dreams because of my confusion, and to this day I have not asked anyone about these dreams. I am clueless with respect to these events. Thus, to this day I continue to block my dreams.

This reaction is not uncommon. I can't tell you how many people I have spoken to over the years who have told me similar things, whether their intuitive gift had expressed itself in dreams or in waking intuitive information. This is so very sad, that a child would turn off his or her intuitive gift out of fear and guilt—and conscientiousness—feeling that he or she had been the one who caused the awful event to happen simply because he or she had foreseen it in some way.

Please take note of this: If you receive precognitive information about a negative event, whether that information comes to you in a dream or while you're awake, and the negative event (whether a plane crash, car accident, someone's death, or whatever) actually does happen, *you have not caused that event to happen.* Period.

An intuitive gift is a wonderful thing. (I cover the topic of intuition fairly comprehensively in my book *Intuition for Beginners.*) We can receive intuitive information about many different types of things, including a future negative event.

I had several people tell me after the awful events of September 11th took place that they had gotten information on them prior to that day, even though they didn't know what it was about.

Intuition is a gift—a gift to be treasured and nurtured and developed.

That said, if you're primarily receiving precognitive information about negative events, whether in a dream or awake, that may not feel good. It may feel uncomfortable. And for a child, it will be even more unpleasant.

So here's what I told the person who shared the previous dream experiences from his childhood: You can actually ask for how you want to be worked with, meaning you can ask to have precognitive or psychic dreams that aren't about negative things and only have positive ones. This applies to having precognitive dreams, intuitive dreams, and intuitive information received while you're awake.

Children, especially, are very vulnerable and sensitive. I feel that children really need guidance from caring, supportive, and knowledgeable adults. So if you know a child who is particularly intuitive or psychic, please let that child know that he or she can ask for how he or she wants to be worked with, that intuition is a special gift, and that you support the child with his or her gift. That could make a world of difference in determining whether the child shuts off the gift or embraces and develops it.

The person who shared the previous dream did not immediately reply to what I had written. However, after a couple of weeks he wrote that he had needed time to process what I had shared with him. He was happy to report that he has now welcomed his dreams back into his life and looks forward to the insights they will give him.

So don't forget that you can ask for how you want to be worked with. You can ask to have positive, helpful dreams and should then find yourself having them.

Actual Experiences and Exploring, Including Past-Life Memories

We've already touched upon the fact that some dreams are actual experiences rather than dreams *about* things. If we're communicating telepathically with someone else, that is an actual experience. However, in addition to that type of real experience, we can also be off exploring other places geographically, such as the Louvre Museum in Paris, and even other time periods, both past and future. Some people feel that they astral-travel (also called an out-of-body experience, in which we have an astral body that travels and explores), but our consciousness can travel and explore other places as well.

I've had two memorable dreams in my lifetime that I still recall and that I feel were from past lives. In one, I was in some ancient temple where I was the priestess and I levitated while speaking to the congregants. In the other, I seemed to be somewhere in the Middle Ages and cautioned others about opening something like a cabinet due to my concern that "the bad humors" would be let out. When I awakened from these dreams, I immediately knew that these had not been my typical, garden-variety types of dreams and that they had been from older time periods.

As mentioned earlier, we may also be doing healing work on others or helping them in some way while we're sleeping, whether this is in the deeper levels of sleep or in dreams. Some people have a conscious awareness of having done this.

These dream experiences usually come from our unconscious and sometimes from other people. That we can have actual experiences in dreams speaks to the beautiful complexity of them.

Recurring Dreams, Including Serial Dreams

We discussed recurring dreams in chapter 2. To briefly reiterate, recurring dreams are those that happen over and over again, whether during a shorter period of weeks or months or over a longer period of years. We can also have dreams that are connected to each other in a series, even if their content is different.

Recurring dreams are often trying to give us a message about something, whether about something that will take place in the future or even from a past life or about a long-standing issue. These dreams often stem from our unconscious, a guide, or our higher soul awareness, and will frequently shift and evolve in content over time.

We often will not know what a recurring dream is trying to tell us if it has to do with a future event. However, if it deals with an unresolved issue from our past—whether in the present lifetime or a past life—we can work on resolving and healing the issue.

Recurring dreams are usually significant in some way, although the onus is on us to determine what the meanings are.

Spiritual Dreams, Including Awakening or Opening Dreams

Spiritual dreams are a very special type of dream. They are actually dreams that appear to be constructed to elicit spiritual insight, awakening, or growth in the dreamer or to open the dreamer to growth. They are usually given to us by a guide or our higher soul awareness, and they may have different types of scenarios frequently populated with spiritual personages, whether guides, angels, priests, priestesses, or other types.

Spiritual dreams may incorporate various kinds of out-of-the-ordinary phenomena, such as levitation, out-of-body experiences, etc. They may also incorporate messages given to us by spiritual entities or spiritual insights, whether conveyed via messages, visual images, sudden insights, and so on. In some, we may be taken to other levels or dimensions to experience things or be taught or given lessons. Because we are more open and receptive and our consciousness is more porous while we're sleeping, especially in the deeper levels of sleep, it is easier for guides and spiritual beings to get through to us, convey information to us, and work with us.

This type of dream is not the norm, and not everyone will have one that is remembered. I had a significant one many years ago, when I was in my twenties, that was part of a series of dream experiences. I was in graduate school at the time and shared an apartment with a roommate who was also in graduate school (the same person I mentioned earlier). I was sound asleep one night when I heard a voice call my name. This led to a spontaneous out-of-body experience, which scared me and made me slam back into my body.

Later that same night, I had another dream in which I was describing my prior dream, with the out-of-body experience, to some older women, whom I knew to be guides. I shared with them that I'd had a dream two weeks prior in which I was told that something significant would happen on the night of the full moon. These ladies/guides then told me that it had been a test.

This set of dreams has never left me. I felt for years that the guides (the elderly ladies) had been referring to the dream experiences being a test of my psychic or spiritual ability. And for years afterward, I felt that I must have failed the test, given my fear of being out of my body. In retrospect, I now feel that the dream experiences served to open me to experiential spiritual experiences. Prior to that night, my knowledge had primarily been just that: cognitive knowledge (aside from my spiritual thoughts, awareness, and memories at birth). So these dream experiences opened me up for more experiential exploring and also possibly to my becoming more consciously aware of being guided and led, and possibly to my working professionally with my intuition. (Interestingly, I have not consciously had another out-of-body experience since then.)

Spiritual awakening or opening dreams feel as if they are being given to us. They come to us without warning or much preparation, and they appear to exist simply to open us up or prepare us for more growth or to give us profound spiritual information or insights. They are a special type of dream and a wonderful gift.

Combinations of Types

As you read the descriptions of the various types of dreams, you may have wondered whether a dream could possibly fit into more than one category.

Yes, it could! The boundaries between and among the various categories of dreams are permeable, and a dream can indeed be a combination of two or more types.

A communication dream could also be considered to be an actual experience. Likewise, you could have a dream that's expressing or working on a personal issue that also contains clairvoyant or precognitive information.

So allow yourself to take this into consideration in working with your dreams, and don't forget that a dream can be a combination of types.

———

You've learned about the different sources of dreams and types of dreams. Now let's look at some of the more common dreams people have and what they could mean.

four

Some Common Dreams and Their Potential Meanings

There are some dreams that are fairly common, which we'll look at next. It's important to note, however, that these dreams, while somewhat common, will probably have different meanings for different people. It's crucial in learning to work with your dreams to uncover the specific meanings your dreams are giving you for your life, as opposed to generic possible meanings or universal ones, because we all have our own vocabulary in our dreams. The meaning of a dream for me may be quite different from what the same dream may mean for you.

These general dream scenarios that are somewhat universal to most people could have a range of different possible meanings, depending upon the person who had the dream and even what the person is experiencing in his or her life when the dream occurs, as well as details and variations in the dream. This is a crucial point to remember, because even a small detail or word in a dream could be laden with personal meaning for the dreamer.

As we go over some of these common dreams, don't fall into the trap of thinking that they will always have any one meaning. We'll go over some of their possible meanings, although these meanings won't be exhaustive, as they will depend upon the person who had them and the other details in the dream.

Interestingly, many, although not all, of the most common dreams are nightmares. This may be due to the fact that striking dreams are the ones we remember, and dreams that elicit strong emotions—and especially negative emotions such as fear—tend to be more memorable ones.

Bear in mind that we all have dreams with uncommon scenarios—scenarios that are specific to us and to our lives—so the following compilation of common dreams is hardly exhaustive. These dreams are simply more common ones. (When we cover specific dreams later on, you'll see how uncommon and individualistic some dreams can be.)

We'll go over these common dreams in no particular order, so a common dream listed first would not be indicative of it being more common. We'll start with common dreams that are usually nightmares and bad dreams rather than pleasant ones.

Nightmares and Bad Dreams

Nightmares often reflect underlying fears and anxieties that we have, even if we're not consciously aware of them. You can use this type of dream as a tool for personal unfolding by working on healing any fears or other issues that nightmares reveal to you.

Some nightmares, on the other hand, may be precognitive and could reveal difficult scenarios that will happen in the future. It's difficult to know whether a dream is precognitive right after having it, because it's often only with the passage of time and an event actually happening that we can then realize that a dream was indeed precognitive. As an illustration of this, consider the fact that many people had dreams before September 11, 2001, that appeared to presage those awful events. At the time that they had these dreams, many people didn't know what they were about; but after the terrible events of that day unfolded, they knew in retrospect that their dreams had been precognitive ones. Interestingly, horrific events that affect a large number of people may be picked up on in advance by more people due to their emotional charge and their significance in our general or collective psyche.

In addition, as I shared earlier, nightmares can also serve as a relief valve, releasing any underlying fears, anxieties, or worries that we may have.

This is one tricky aspect of dealing with some nightmares: determining whether the dream was literal and precognitive or if it was expressing underlying fears or simply releasing negative feelings. We must determine for ourselves whether a nightmare was about a fear or an actual event that will happen or if it served as a relief valve.

Here are some of the more common nightmares.

Dreams in Which You Find Yourself Naked

Although the specific scenario can vary, in this type of dream you are usually out somewhere in public, possibly with people around you, and you notice that you don't have any clothes on. This dream could indicate that you may be feeling vulnerable, inadequate, exposed, inconsequential, ridiculed, defenseless, without everyday artifice, that you have no secrets, that you feel small or ganged up on by others, etc. It's usually not a pleasant dream and doesn't usually elicit pleasant feelings.

There can be exceptions, however, to these possible meanings. For example, if you're a nudist, you might enjoy the dream. If you feel good in the dream, then it wouldn't be a nightmare and there may be other meanings, such as starting a new, fresh phase in your life in which you're shedding everything you used to do or the habits you used to "wear"; or in the dream you may be around people you've been getting closer to, with the effect that the dream could indicate that you're getting closer to them and don't mind "baring your soul" or showing them who you are on a deeper level.

As you can see, there are several different possible meanings of a dream like this, depending upon the actual scenario in the dream, the feelings elicited, and what's going on in your life.

Dreams in Which You're Being Chased

In this type of nightmare, you find yourself running away because you're being chased. You could be chased by another person, a marauder with evil intent, or even an animal, such as a ferocious tiger. Sometimes people have recurring dreams of being chased. You may wake up with your heart pounding and feel afraid.

So what could this type of nightmare mean?

Dreams in which you're being chased and you're fearful during them could mean that you're feeling overwhelmed in some way or by something, that you're very stressed (your to-do list is "pursuing" you, for example), that something you may be avoiding is catching up with you, or that you're not getting something done in your life that you feel you should. Nightmares like this could also indicate that you feel that you're surrounded by negative people who are hounding you or out to get you.

It's important to consider who or what is chasing you in nightmares like these, as that can give insight into meanings.

I should note that it's also possible to have dreams in which you're being chased that are not nightmares. Once when I was speaking to a group about dreams, a woman in the audience shared that she had recurring dreams of being chased. The first thing that I—as well as other audience members—thought was that these must have been nightmares. However, when I asked her how she felt in the dreams, she replied that they were pleasant and that she enjoyed them. For her, these dreams were obviously not nightmares. This points to how important it is to consider the feelings elicited by a dream when trying to interpret it. What you feel during a dream—and even upon awakening—can give you insight into meanings, just as this example shows.

Dreams in Which You Have to Take a Test and Feel Unprepared or Fail It

Have you ever had a dream in which you were taking a test that you were worried about flunking because you hadn't studied, or one in which you were taking a test and failing it? If you have, you're definitely not alone! This is another very common dream that borders on being a nightmare, depending upon the intensity of the negative feelings it elicits and whether it awakens you.

As you might suspect, this type of nightmare can indicate that you feel unprepared in some way or that you haven't done something correctly. It can also reflect your feeling that you have to prove yourself in some way, while also feeling inadequate or in the dark about what you are to do. You might ask yourself how or in what ways you're being "tested" in your life.

There are variations on this scenario, in that you might have similar nightmares about being unprepared but not in the context or scenario of taking a test. For example, I've had a variation on this intermittently over the years. I sometimes have a dream in which I'm in a play that is due to open and I've never been to a rehearsal and/or haven't looked at the script and don't know my lines. (I did theatre for many years, so this type of scenario springs from my background.) While I'm not dreaming about taking a test, the thrust of the dream is the same: worry about being unprepared or worry about not "performing" well.

Regardless of the scenario—whether taking a test in a classroom or having to perform well on stage—the meaning of the dream may be the same: that of a fear of lack of preparation and an inability to prove oneself.

On the other hand, what if you enjoy taking tests? If that's the case and you have a dream like this, you may be looking for new ways in which to prove yourself.

Dreams in Which Your Teeth Are Falling Out or Missing

In your dream, you notice that a front tooth has come out or even that all of your teeth are falling out or that your teeth are rotting. Obviously this type of dream doesn't usually elicit good feelings. So what could dreams—or nightmares—like these mean?

A dream like this may be expressing a fear of losing control or even a fear of aging. It could also be reflecting a feeling of being unattractive or fear of losing your looks. It may be expressing a fear of being prevented from eating or a fear of being hungry or not having food. It could also be expressing a fear of a fall from grace or tumbling from a position of power—or of not being able to speak or assert yourself.

Some people feel that this type of nightmare may be expressing a lack of power, because teeth allow us to bite, tear, and chew. I'm not convinced of this, but I can't rule it out.

As always, it's important to look at the entire scenario of a dream in detail and take into account what is going on in the life of the person who had the dream before drawing conclusions about meanings. Dialoguing with the dreamer about this could elicit a different meaning altogether.

A variation in the scenario could also result in an entirely different meaning. For example, if you had this dream before you were going to have major dental work done, the dream might reflect not only the dental work or your fear of undergoing it, but also possibly a new phase or revamping of something in your life.

Dreams in Which You're Drowning

You're in the water struggling. Your head keeps going below the surface. You struggle to breathe. Ever had a nightmare like this?

Nightmares of drowning are not uncommon. They could indicate that you're feeling overwhelmed or that you're exerting yourself without any return on your efforts. They could also reflect a fear of water or even a past-life memory of having drowned. There could be figurative meanings as well, such as feeling that you're figuratively "drowning" in something, such as a large amount of work, too many demands on you, or even too much candy over the holidays. It could also mean that's something flowing too much in your life (such as money flowing out or unfilled time, for example) or that there's no feeling of solid ground under you.

The potential meanings will be dependent upon the exact scenario of the nightmare and your own personal connotations with the symbols and what is going on in your life. If you're drowning along with other people in the water who are also drowning, it could mean something else, such as a group effort or project not going well or being overwhelming. If someone is actually holding you under the water and trying to drown you, another meaning would emerge, such as betrayal or someone trying to get at you. Remember that meanings will vary according to a dream's entire scenario.

Whereas some people may feel that water always symbolizes emotions and that a drowning dream may symbolize a feeling of drowning in feelings, I am not at all convinced of this—unless that meaning resonates with the dreamer. Look for personal—not universal—meanings!

If you have a dream like this and realize that you felt good during the dream, other meanings could emerge. It could be that you love water and need to spend some time in it, or that you're feeling bored in your life and are looking for a new project to totally "immerse" yourself in.

Dreams in Which You're Lost

What happens in nightmares like this may vary, but you basically find yourself lost. You're trying to get somewhere, although the destination can vary, but you can't find your way. You may also have trouble getting or following directions or getting help from anyone. You may simply feel lost, or you may find yourself in a scary place with menacing people and you can't find your way out.

Dreams in which the dreamer is lost may be worse for children than for adults, but anyone can have this type of dream, irrespective of age. Being lost can be terribly frightening for children but less so for adults, unless the dream scenario itself is scary—filled with thugs or killers or menacing people, for example.

Being lost in a dream may reflect a feeling of not being in control in life or a feeling of not knowing what to do next. It could also mean that the dreamer is conflicted about his or her direction in life, whether in terms of career, relationship, life purpose, or any other area of life. It can also be communicating a feeling of "not being able to find one's way" in a figurative sense. Another potential meaning would be that of feeling that you don't pay attention or you're not correctly following directions, reflecting a negative self-judgment.

Should you have a dream in which you're lost and yet you feel good in the dream, other meanings could be implicit. For example, the dream could be telling you that you've been too focused and that you need to "lose yourself" in something recreational. Remember that small details in a dream can give clues as to meanings.

Dreams in Which Your Car Breaks Down or Is Out of Control

Dreams in which your car breaks down or is lurching out of control are also not uncommon. You might find yourself waking up from one and be shaking with fear. We all tend to fear having a car accident. However, this type of dream may not necessarily be about a car accident.

A car is often how we get to places in our lives, so our car in a dream may be a metaphor for this. Dreams in which our car breaks down or is out of control may be reflecting a feeling of not being able to move forward in life, or of things in our lives being out of control, or our not being able to control where we're headed.

Again, this scenario could vary, and it's important to look at all the details in a dream in order to derive complete meanings.

If you felt good during a dream like this, then it's obviously not a nightmare. Your dream may be telling you that you've been too focused or controlled in your life and need to lighten up and let yourself be a little "out of control," or that you may have been working too hard for too long and need a vacation in which you can allow yourself to loosen up.

Never forget that feelings in a dream and even small details will have a huge bearing on meanings.

Dreams in Which You're Falling

There are different falling scenarios in dreams. In one, you may be lying in bed just thinking of different things. You would swear that you're awake and just thinking, then all of a sudden you feel like you're falling and you jerk awake.

This is one possible scenario of a dream in which you're falling. This is not necessarily a nightmare, though, and it's not at all uncommon. It's usually indicative of having been in what is called the "hypnagogic" state, which is a state of consciousness. When we go to sleep, as we covered in chapter 1, our brain waves slow down and we gradually descend into the sleeping state of consciousness. The hypnagogic state is the state between being awake and sleeping. It's one in which we feel as if we're still awake, but our brain and body chemicals have already been in the process of switching over to those of the sleeping state. In actuality, our mind has also been transitioning to the sleeping state. The telltale sign is the feeling of falling and jerking back to being awake.

There are other fairly common falling dreams that are not reflective of having been in a hypnagogic state. Have you ever dreamed that you were falling to your death? I haven't, but this is not an uncommon dream. So what could it mean?

Dreams in which you're falling from a cliff or falling into an abyss could be reflecting a fear of heights, a fear of not being in control (and thus free-falling with nothing to hold on to), or even a fear of death. It could also be expressing a feeling of having no support in life and nothing to fall back on or hold on to.

When we vary the feeling elicited in a dream like this, other meanings could emerge. Let's say you find yourself on a cliff, holding on, and then you fall off. You find yourself feeling good as you're falling. What could it mean? It could indicate that you need to let go in some way in your life, rather than rigidly holding on to something (a work project, career, relationship, etc.). You know by now that one simple change, such as the feeling elicited by a dream, can yield entirely different meanings.

Dreams in Which You're Being Attacked

You're sleeping and people are attacking you. You try to get away, but you can't. You wake up sweating and afraid.

Yes, this is yet another somewhat common dream. What could it possibly mean? Could it mean that in the not-so-distant future some people will actually attack you?

No, not necessarily. Again, we can't rule out that a dream like this might be precognitive, but in most cases it won't be.

Having dreams in which you're attacked by others could reflect a fear of others or of strangers, a fear of people suddenly turning on you, a fear of not fitting in, a fear of being negatively judged, a fear of things or people not being predictable, a literal fear of violence for some reason, or a fear of being criticized or figuratively attacked by others. It's important to remember that our dreams are not always literal and are, instead, often figurative or symbolic.

Details in the scenario will yield clues to possible meanings. How are the people attacking you in the dream? Is it with swords or lethal weapons, or is it with something innocuous, such as wet noodles or balloons? The varying details will give different meanings. If you're being attacked by a lethal weapon, then the dream may be saying that someone is trying to kill you or something in you, such as a personal trait. If you're being attacked by wet noodles or balloons, there may be no negative intent, but rather a more humorous intention or teasing.

Did you enjoy the experience of being attacked? If so, different meanings will emerge, including needing a challenge coming from others, thriving on competition, or even teaming up with others for self-growth opportunities or good-natured sparring or sports.

Looking at the entire dream scenario in detail should give you more clues as to its meaning and what, if anything, you might need to do in real life with information gleaned from the dream.

Dreams in Which You Have a Serious Illness

Have you ever had a dream in which you had a serious illness—cancer, for example? People do have dreams like this on occasion. We might not consider them outright to be nightmares, but they may not be pleasant.

Dreams like this could reflect a fear of something unknown negatively affecting you out of the blue or even a fear of illness or a fear of contracting a serious disease. They could also be expressing a fear of not being able to enjoy your life or not being able to move forward in life, or even possibly of there being something wrong ("ill" or "rotten") in your life.

If a dream like this is not expressing an underlying fear, it could be giving you a message: that you may actually have the illness you dreamed about or one like it. Remember that there have been people who have dreamed they had an illness—breast cancer, for example—that they were unaware of having, and who later had the diagnosis confirmed through medical tests.

If a dream about having an illness feels real to you, it wouldn't hurt to follow it up with a doctor's appointment. If it's not a literal dream with a real message about a health condition, then you'll want to look at any fear or worry that your dream may be expressing to you.

If you feel good in the dream, other meanings will emerge. Let's say you dream that you're sick in bed, but you feel good in the dream. What could that mean? If you've been working harder than usual and have been longing for some time off, your dream could be expressing that, even if you have to get sick in order to get that time off. It could also mean that you need some nurturing or TLC.

Strong, memorable dreams will often give us messages that can be useful in our lives, once we decode their meanings.

Dreams in Which You Have Marbles or Other Things in Your Mouth and Can't Speak

You're talking to a group of friends or even giving a speech and suddenly you realize that your mouth is full of marbles or cotton and that you can't speak as a result. What could a dream like this mean?

Again, depending upon whether you feel good or bad in the dream, different meanings will emerge. If you feel bad during a dream like this, the dream could be expressing a fear of not being able to speak or express yourself or state an opinion. It could also represent a fear of being inadequate in a social situation or of not being able to communicate with others. If you tend to be a little fearful in social settings or if your friends tend to be highly educated and articulate, your dream could be expressing a fear of being seen as inadequate or inarticulate.

On the other hand, if you feel good in the dream, other meanings could be valid. Your dream may be expressing a desire not to have to communicate with some people or that you're tired of expressing your opinion or thoughts and want to avoid having to do so, or it could even be precognitive and foretelling your not having to speak about a topic you may not want to talk about.

Allow yourself to look at all the details in your dream in order to piece together your dream's meanings for you.

Dreams in Which You Find Yourself Paralyzed

You're sleeping and all of a sudden you feel yourself paralyzed. You find it hard to move and may struggle to do so.

A dream like this could mean a number of things. If you'll recall what we discussed about dreams of falling, you'll remember that your brain and body chemicals change as you fall asleep and that sometimes falling dreams can result from waking up during the hypnagogic state.

A similar thing happens on the other end of the sleep cycle, when we wake up. Our brain and body chemicals change back to those of the waking state. This process of waking up is called the hypnopompic state. If we try to wake up before those chemicals have changed, we may feel that we can't move and feel paralyzed. This is a mundane cause of some dreams in which you find yourself paralyzed.

If your dream is not occurring as you are waking up in the morning, then it could have other meanings. If you were scared during the dream, it could indicate a fear of being paralyzed or even a literal "paralyzing fear." It could also represent a fear of being in a coma or a fear of activities that would be physically challenging, such as rock climbing, or a fear of being physically limited for some reason. It could indicate a fear of being called upon to do something and not being able to do it.

You would need to examine the entire dream scenario and all the details therein to get fuller and perhaps different meanings. For example, if you were with a group of people in your dream and you were supposed to be doing or saying something for the group, being paralyzed could represent a fear of performing well or even of feeling intimidated by the particular people around you.

What if you feel good during a dream like this? In that case, your dream could indicate that there's something you don't want to do, and being prevented from doing it feels good—or, if there's a project you want to spend more time on, the dream could be indicating that it would be good to feel frozen in time so that you will have more time to devote to the project or planning it.

As always, look at all the details in your dream before deriving any meanings.

Dreams of People Who Are Dead

Dreaming of people who are deceased is not at all uncommon, and there are several possible meanings of such dreams.

If the dream was a nightmare, it could indicate a fear of death, or a fear of being around corpses, or even a fear of figurative death—i.e., things changing substantially in your life. Perhaps the dream was of a passed-on loved one and it felt like a nightmare to you. Were there unresolved issues with that person, or were you fearful of the person in real life? If so, the dream could be indicating that those negative issues are still "haunting" you or that your fear of the person didn't "die" with the person's passing.

Even if you were fearful during the dream or when you woke up, the dream may not have been a true nightmare. The person may have actually been trying to communicate with you, rather than your having dreamed *about* the person. People who have passed on will often try to communicate to loved ones still in body that they're all right. They may try to communicate with us while we're awake, perhaps by whispering to us or trying to physically appear to us, or even by communicating the scent of their customary perfume or cologne to us. If they feel stymied in doing this because we're not aware of the communication or are blocking it for some reason, they will sometimes try to get through to us while we're sleeping, by communicating with us then or by appearing to us in our dreams.

If we have a fear of death or dead people, this may not feel good and we may be fearful. If we truly miss the person and aren't fearful, this type of communication or visitation can feel quite pleasant. We may feel reassured by realizing that our loved one is still "with us" and hasn't truly gone away. We can also be given useful and comforting information by a loved one in dreams like this.

As you can see, how you felt in a dream like this can yield varying results. If we're open to life after death, we may find dreams like this to be very positive and reassuring.

The following are common dreams that are not nightmares.

Dreams in Which You're Flying

Flying dreams are one of the most common dreams, and they're usually pleasant, although the actual mode of flying can vary from one person to another. I've had flying dreams off and on over the years and love them. Other people have similarly told me that they love their flying dreams.

In my flying dreams, I basically flap my arms as if they were wings and pedal my legs and find myself lifting off the ground and flying. Sometimes I just make a mental effort and lift upward and look down at the people and other things below. Many people may just float upward. Even though the actual physical mode of flying may vary from one person to the next, there is usually a pleasant feeling evoked by flying, even euphoria.

Many people who are spiritual feel that flying dreams express how we feel when we're not in a body and can move about at will. In more mundane terms, flying dreams can express a feeling of not being weighed down or restricted, a state of pure liberation and freedom of movement.

Depending upon the scenario of the dream and the details in it, other meanings can emerge. For example, if you find yourself floating upward and easily flying around while other people remain on the ground, your dream could be expressing a sense of having abilities or a freedom or even a higher vantage point that others don't have.

Flying dreams are wonderful and to be enjoyed, at least as long as they don't elicit negative feelings. If you have a flying dream that feels unpleasant, it could be indicating a fear of letting go, or a fear of not having something substantial to hold on to, or a fear of not having solid ground under your feet.

If it feels pleasant, allow yourself to enjoy your flying dreams!

Dreams in Which You're Pregnant or Giving Birth

Many people have dreams from time to time in which they're pregnant or in labor and giving birth to a baby. While a dream like this could be a nightmare if fear or negative feelings were elicited during it, it's not usually a nightmare.

Dreams like this could be literal and expressing a desire to have a baby. They could also be precognitive and foretelling getting pregnant or how labor will go.

However, this type of dream could also be symbolic, in which case it may often be indicating that something new is coming into our lives. Often this dream will be expressing either a need for a new project to throw ourselves into or that we will soon have a new project. If we're already working on a big project at work, this type of dream could be expressing the outcome. A successful birth with a healthy baby, for example, would indicate a successful completion of the project.

Bathroom Dreams

I came up with this phrase some years ago after observing my own dreams of this nature. I would be sleeping and trying to find a bathroom in my dream, or I'd head to a public restroom and there would be a long line or none of the toilets would be working. (I've had many variations on this scenario, the common thread being the need to urinate and being delayed in trying to do so.) I would then wake up from my dream and discover that I did indeed need to get to the bathroom.

After discussing this type of dream with others over the years, I have come to realize that I'm not alone. Many people have "bathroom dreams." Dreams like this may not be full of meaning for us, but they definitely give us a message. Acknowledging that bathroom dreams are fairly common can help us remember, when we have one, that there's a bodily need that needs to be attended to!

We've examined some common dreams and nightmares. Next we'll begin to learn how to interpret and understand our dreams.

part 2

How to Interpret and Understand Your Dreams

five

Tips for Interpreting Your Dreams and a Step-by-Step Procedure

Now let's get down to the nitty-gritty of how to understand your dreams. In this chapter you'll learn a step-by-step procedure for interpreting your dreams, but first I'll share some tips and recommendations for understanding your dreams.

Tip #1: If a Dream Isn't Significant, Don't Spend Your Time on It

Many of us may feel that dreams are always pure events, emerging from a wellspring of wisdom within us, and are thus to be revered. Well, aside from the fact there are numerous different sources of dreams, some dreams are just not significant.

There are several things that can intrude upon and affect our dream content, as we covered earlier. These triggers can include our physical condition, our mental/emotional condition, and what I call the ambient energy (the general energy that is affected by our world zeitgeist and what may be going on in our world). For example, if you have a fever, your sleep quality will be different and the dreams you have will likely be affected as well. Likewise, bathroom dreams in which you are trying to get to a restroom (and toilet) will stem from your bladder being full. This type of dream will likely not be significant in content for you, other than its signaling to you the need to wake up and attend to your bladder.

Because our dreams are not always pure events, not all of our dreams will be significant. I recommend that you work with interpreting only those dreams that are significant and not every dream that you have.

We typically know that a dream was significant because we sense that it was. It may elicit strong emotions in us, or we may be struck by how bizarre it seemed, or we may have trouble getting it out of our minds. It is this type of dream that you want to spend your time understanding and working on, as it will likely yield the most helpful information for you.

Tip #2: Keep a Dream Journal and Review It Regularly

This is probably the best known method of working with dreams, and we touched upon it earlier in chapter 2. A dream journal is simply a way of recording your dreams. It's much easier to interpret a dream if you've written it down, and you can also use your dream journal for intermittent review of your dreams. You'll want to record only your significant dreams, and you don't want to interrupt your sleep in order to record each one.

Once you determine that a dream was significant, write it down in your journal from beginning to end in full detail. You'll want to do this as quickly as possible after waking up, because our dreams evaporate so quickly. (Remember that we typically forget 50 percent of a dream within five minutes of waking up and 90 percent within ten minutes.)

You can write your dreams down on a notepad that can serve as your dream journal, or you can dictate them into a handheld digital recorder and transfer them later to a hand-written dream journal or a typed file on your computer. Some people like to record their dreams in an artistic-looking journal, while others may use any type of notebook. Whatever you decide to use is up to you, of course, although if your dream journal is aesthetically pleasing and beautiful, it could remind you to value your dreams even more and regard them as a beautiful gift.

Review your dreams every now and then. Often when we reread a dream we had several months earlier, we'll have a better sense of what it was about, the information it gave us, and how we may have shifted and evolved since that time. This can also give us a better sense of what our dreaming world is like, as well as our own particular style of dreaming.

Dream journals are very useful, and I invite you to use one!

Tip #3: Remember That Not All Dreams Are Symbolic

We may feel that every dream will be laden with symbols that we need to work at interpreting and understanding. Fortunately this is not true. There are some dreams that are straightforward and literal.

So how do you know whether a dream was symbolic or literal?

Once again, the onus is on you to determine whether a dream was literal or symbolic—or even literal *and* symbolic. One general rule of thumb, though, is that the more bizarre a dream seems and the more it has you scratching your head over it, the more likely it is to be fraught with symbols.

If a dream is precognitive, it's more likely that it will be literal. However, remember that we usually only know that a dream was indeed precognitive after the dreamed-of event actually takes place—*and* it's always possible that a dream that is heavily laden with symbols could also be precognitive. Dreams can be beautifully complex, and anything is possible.

Lest this discourage you, please know that you can learn how to interpret and work with your dreams, and this discussion merely speaks to the beautiful complexity of them. Dreams are remarkable events to be respected!

The bottom line is that dream interpretation is a skill that can be learned. You may find yourself feeling your way along initially with dream interpretation, but your ability and expertise should grow over time, and the rewards are huge!

For now, just remember that not all dreams are symbolic and that some are both symbolic and literal.

Tip #4: Respect Your Dreams

You wake up from a vivid dream and find yourself thinking, "That was such a bizarre dream! It was so bizarre that surely it can't mean anything." I've often had others tell me this when they have a dream they want me to interpret. Unfortunately, the bizarre nature of some dreams leads some people to feel not only that their dreams have no true meaning or significance, but also that their dreams should be disregarded and dismissed.

Yes, many dreams will seem bizarre. However, even though they may be bizarre, they will usually make perfect sense once you tease out their meanings. What can get in the way of your finding the right interpretations for your dreams, though, will often be your attitude toward them.

If you feel that a dream of yours was really bizarre, you'll want to make sure that you still respect it. If you find yourself having a derogatory attitude toward your dream simply because it seemed bizarre, this could be a block to your being able to mine the riches from it.

So the best way to approach your dreams—including the very bizarre ones—is with an attitude of respect. Remind yourself that your dream may seem bizarre because it's cloaked in symbolism that you haven't yet decoded—and that once you're able to do that, the full richness of your dream will be revealed to you.

Tip #5: Pay Attention to How You Feel

In working on understanding our dreams, we often focus primarily on the symbols in them and on trying to figure out their meanings. We may feel that this is the sole thing to look at in interpreting our dreams. In truth, there are other factors to consider.

How you felt is also critical to understanding your dreams—how you felt during the dream, upon awakening, and even in retrospect.

You may recall the example I gave earlier of the woman who had recurring dreams about being chased. Whereas we would normally think that this type of dream would be a nightmare, the key to determining whether it was or not is how she felt in it. Remember that she didn't feel afraid—or anxious—or tense. If she had, her recurring dreams would have been bad ones or nightmares. Instead, she enjoyed them. They were pleasant for her.

So the type of emotion you feel can be key and a clue to understanding a dream or even different parts of a dream. You may feel different things at different points in your dream, or you may feel something different upon awakening.

Always remember to include your feelings as factors that can point to what your dream meant.

Tip #6: Wake Up Slowly

Remember that you forget most of your dreams within a few minutes of waking up. As soon as you open your eyes, your consciousness is bombarded with stimuli and you start focusing on your present surroundings, losing touch with your inner world. Your outer world truly takes over as the center of your attention.

Even if the dream you had just before waking up wasn't significant, there may have been important information for you in other dreams you had or parts of your sleep that could be helpful for you.

So allow yourself to wake up slowly with your eyes still closed, as you savor the information from your dreams and sleep. Make mental notes of any important details. Once you've remembered and gleaned as much information and as many sleep and dream memories as you can and made notes, then opening your eyes and moving about is appropriate and won't interfere with your holding on to what was there for you while you were sleeping.

By allowing yourself to wake up slowly and savor important information, you'll be less likely to lose it from your mind.

Tip #7: Try to Determine What Each Symbol in a Dream Means to *You*

Many of our dreams are loaded with symbols that can mask their true meanings, and it's imperative in interpreting dreams with symbols to tease out the correct and relevant meanings.

There's some debate over whether there are simply universal meanings of dream symbols or whether symbols have personal and individual meanings. I feel that for dreams coming from our unconscious, the symbols in those dreams will be individual, personal ones that will have meanings specific for us. Our unconscious has its own vocabulary and works quite differently from our conscious mind. Our unconscious operates by stream of consciousness and association (or connotation).

That said, I have encountered some fairly universal symbols in dreams. For example, a house may symbolize our mind or "where we live." A car may symbolize mobility or where we're headed in life or moving forward. A baby in a dream could signify a literal baby or be figurative, signifying something new in one's life, such as a new project or starting a new phase.

For symbols stemming from our unconscious, it's important that we ask ourselves, "What does this symbol mean to me?" or "What do I think of when I think of (the symbol)?" A symbol in a dream that stems from your unconscious will have *your* meanings for the symbols—your own individual connotations and associations. This is how we mine all the riches from our dreams for ourselves in our lives.

If you're interpreting someone else's dream, allow yourself to dialogue with that person about each symbol's meaning. Just ask the other person, "What do you think of when you think of (the symbol)?" In fact, engaging in dialogue with the dreamer is an important thing to do when you're interpreting someone else's dream.

Several years ago, I had a dream in which there was a box of coins buried in the backyard. If you look up coins as a symbol in a dream dictionary, you will find that the universal meaning is wealth or prosperity. However, at that time in my life, my father was collecting coins. So, for me, the coins in my dream had something to do with my father. I would never have gotten a meaning like that had I just consulted a dream dictionary.

If a dream is springing from your unconscious, you'll want to find the meanings of the symbols in it that are true for you and your mind and connotations. This will give you the truest meanings of the dream for yourself.

Tip #8: Remember That Any One Symbol/Dream Can Have More Than One Valid Meaning

As you approach your dreams for interpretation, you'll want to keep in mind that any one symbol in a dream can have more than one valid meaning. Likewise, any dream can have more than one valid meaning for the person who had it. If you look for just one meaning of a symbol or a whole dream, you may be missing out on additional important meanings.

Tip #9: Pay Attention to Any Puns and Plays on Words

As mentioned previously, your unconscious works quite differently from your conscious mind. Whereas our conscious mind can be linear in its logic and progression, the unconscious works in a nonlinear fashion—by association, connotation, and even images. Perhaps because of this, your unconscious loves puns and plays on words, and they will frequently turn up in dreams.

Let's say that you have a dream with several cats in it. You ask yourself if cats have any particular meaning for you because you don't have a cat. Then you remember that you know someone with the last name of Katz. Could the cats in your dream symbolize the person you know? Yes, this is entirely possible. If you think of the nature of the relationship you have with the person—pleasant, unpleasant, tiring, exploratory, etc.—you'll derive even more meaning from the cats in your dream.

As another example, you may have a dream in which you're trying to pick up a bucket. What could that mean? This could be another pun that derives from a pictorial representation. It could mean that there's something you can't get a handle on. Do you see how that meaning could be derived from not being able to pick up the bucket?

As a third example, you may have a dream in which you're in your car, which is moving, but you're in the back seat. What could that mean? This could mean that you're not in the driver's seat in your life.

With the dream that I shared earlier in which there was a box of coins buried in the backyard, the symbol of coins could also be a pun, meaning that there was something new I was "coining" or going to "coin."

Your unconscious will frequently try to convey the meaning of something through the use of puns, almost as if you or someone in your dream were literally playing out the meaning of a pun through a pictorial representation. Yes, this is a strange concept, as it mixes the literal with the symbolic or metaphoric.

In any case, puns will make frequent appearances in dreams, so it's important to always consider whether a symbol or segment of a dream may be a pun and, if so, what it's conveying.

Tip #10: Pay Attention to Tone, Inflection, and Emphasis

Sometimes we'll get hints at meaning in dreams in very subtle ways. If someone else is telling you his or her dream, there can be nuances in the way a dream is related that will convey meaning or significance. I've noticed over the years that a person's inflection or tone of voice in relating some words or phrases will be different and point to meanings or importance. This can also include words or phrases that may jump out at you or feel different or unusual as you're hearing the dream related. For example, a dreamer may subtly emphasize the word "light" in telling you a dream. You would then know that the light in the dream had some significance.

There's no point-by-point guideline for you in searching for these subtle items of significance. It's a matter of sensing when something feels significant. You'll want to be attuned to subtleties in voices and use your intuition.

This may feel challenging initially. However, over time, your expertise should grow and you should become aware of these subtle added meanings.

Tip #11: Look at Other People in Your Dream

Sometimes other people appearing in our dreams may represent parts of ourselves that are being emphasized for some reason. It could be that a person in your dream is representing a trait that you have that you overlook or don't like in yourself. Let's say that in your dream there's a really rude person who's insulting other people. In looking at this dream character as a part of yourself that you don't like in yourself, your dream may be reminding you that you dislike rudeness so much that you repress it in yourself and may be overly friendly. This could be giving you a message that you could assert yourself more with others.

Similarly, a dream character like this may be indicating that you have a tendency to be rude and may be excusing it in yourself while condemning it in others.

Someone appearing in your dream could also represent a positive characteristic that you have that you don't give yourself credit for. Let's say you have a dream in which a teacher is so good that her students learn material well and do well on tests. This dream may be reminding you that you're a good teacher to others or that you help others in some way.

Looking at other people appearing in our dreams as potential parts of ourselves will often yield even more significant meanings.

Tip #12: Use Your Intuition

One critical tool in interpreting dreams is intuition. I've been interpreting dreams for many years, and intuition is crucial for determining correct meanings of dreams. Intuition will guide you in sensing the meanings of symbols and dreams, and it truly is essential in understanding dreams. It's a tool that can't be overlooked and shouldn't be undervalued.

If you haven't developed your intuition or don't consider yourself to be intuitive, know that this is a skill that can be learned and developed. Just see my book *Intuition for Beginners: Easy Ways to Awaken Your Natural Abilities.* It's a hands-on, how-to guide for accessing your intuition on demand and developing it.

If you learn all the ins and outs of dreams and some steps on how to interpret them but haven't developed your intuition, you're likely not to derive the full meanings of dreams. I can't emphasize enough the importance of intuition.

So allow yourself to develop and fine-tune your intuition, and be sure to employ it.

Tip #13: If You're Interpreting Someone Else's Dream, Dialogue with the Person

Sometimes we may feel that we need to get all the valuable interpretive information about someone else's dream without any input from the other person. This is not true. It's very important to dialogue with the person who had the dream. Not only will you get more insight into the personal meanings of the dream's symbols, but you will also likely get additional information that can shed even more light on the dream's meanings, especially in the context of the person's life and what he or she may be experiencing or dealing with at the time.

You can ask simple questions about the meanings of the symbols, what the dreamer felt like, etc., while also looking for validation and confirmation. You can also ask the dreamer if there has been a relevant situation that he or she has been dealing with of late.

Remember that the goal of interpreting someone else's dream is to yield as much helpful insight and information for that person as possible. Engaging in dialogue with the dreamer will enable you to do this to a much greater degree.

Tip #14: Look for the Valid Meanings for the Dreamer

One thing that I have encountered over and over again when I've spoken about dreams or taught others about them is the tendency to put our own spin on somebody else's dream. Most dreams will have quite personal, individual meanings for the person who had the dream. If we look primarily for what a dream <u>means</u> to us, we will usually overlook what the dream truly means for the dreamer.

If you interpret someone else's dream, remind yourself that it's *not your dream* and not to put your spin on it, and remember that the dream will benefit the dreamer the most once the person understands what it's specifically telling him or her.

How will you know that the interpretation is valid? I have seen repeatedly that when I have helped find the right interpretation of a client's dream, my client will have an aha moment of recognition—because the meanings will resonate. This is the case for most types of dreams, except precognitive ones. So look for an aha!

A Procedure for Interpreting Dreams

Next we'll go over a specific step-by-step procedure for interpreting dreams and for remembering and recording them. This procedure builds on everything we've covered and will guide you through the process. Keep all the previous tips in mind as you interpret dreams using this procedure.

1. **Ask yourself what type of dream it is and whether it's significant or not.**

   As we've touched upon before, not every dream will be significant for you, so you don't want to take time to painstakingly examine every dream. Significant dreams will have more meaning for you, and it's these dreams that you'll want to pay attention to and interpret.

   You'll also remember that there are different sources and types of dreams. Determining which type (or combination of types) of dream it was will give you clues as to its meaning. For example, a dream that was about filing away mundane events from the day may not be as significant as a dream in which a passed-on loved one gave you a message.

2. **Ask yourself how you felt in the dream. How did you feel upon awakening, and how do you feel in retrospect?**

   Remember that various feelings and emotions can give you clues as to meanings in dreams. When working with dreams, you'll always want to take into consideration your feelings in the dream and about the dream.

3. **Review the dream in detail from beginning to end in a very relaxed state of consciousness, and see what goes through your mind as you do this. If it's another person's dream, ask the person to relate the dream to you in detail, from beginning to end. This is especially where you can use your intuition.**

This is an important step in starting to grasp meanings in the dream. Sometimes meanings and associations will flash through your mind as the dream is reviewed. It's crucial to be in a relaxed frame of mind as you do this and to use your intuition.

It's also important that the dream be related in as much detail as possible from beginning to end. Sometimes people will want to just summarize a dream when sharing it for interpretation. No twenty-five words or less summaries! Often the smallest detail in a dream will have meaning, and you won't get that in a quick summary.

So remember to review the entire dream in detail as it unfolded.

4. **Begin to look at every symbol in a dream and decode it, remembering that it could have more than one valid meaning.**

This can be detailed work and it may take some time, especially if it's a longer dream. You'll want to go over every symbol in the dream and decode its meanings. No matter how bizarre the symbols may be, they should have valid meanings once you've accurately teased them out. If you refer to a dream dictionary, don't fall into the trap of thinking that you'll have found all the valid meanings, as you'll need to look for personal ones.

5. **Look for any prominent words or phrases, as well as any puns and plays on words and pictorial representations. Then look for their meanings.**

   Remember that your unconscious loves puns and plays on words and loves to draw pictures, and that these could have significant meanings in your dreams. If you have trouble finding any, don't forget to employ your intuition, as it will frequently hone in on them with a laser-like focus.

6. **Look at other people appearing in your dream and ask if they could represent parts of yourself.**

   Remember that sometimes other people appearing in our dreams may signify parts of us or personal characteristics of ours. They may thus serve as symbols for us. You'll want to determine what each person represents.

   Remember to tease out any significant meaning for each person in your dream.

7. **Look for any elements of your dream that may have particular significance for you and then tease out their meanings.**

   If we have a strong interest in something, elements connected to it may turn up in our dreams. For example, an artist might dream of colors or a numerologist might dream of numbers. If these elements have symbolic significance for you, you'll want to determine what they mean in the context of the dream, as they may be adding layers of meaning or nuance to your dream.

8. **Ask yourself what the general theme of the dream is and what area of your life it relates to.**

    Because significant dreams will often give us important information for our lives, we need to determine which area of our life it's pertaining to. This could be the career area, for example, or family or creativity or a romantic relationship. In addition, you'll want to get a sense of what the general theme of the dream is. Is it, for example, warning you about a problem with a new job or relationship, or is it giving you insight into someone else in your life?

    At this point, this information about the dream will likely be fairly general rather than the full interpretation of the dream.

9. **Now break the dream down into its various story segments, especially if it's a long dream. This will be like storyboarding the dream and breaking it down according to each smaller scenario. Then work with each segment to figure out its full meaning.**

    This step is especially helpful to do with longer dreams. Remember that some dreams can be fairly short (as little as four minutes), while others can be much longer and more involved (as many as seventy-two minutes). Trying to work with a long dream all at once can be overwhelming, so breaking it down into its story segments can help.

    Then take each dream segment and determine what it means, referring back to each symbol that you decoded. Keep working with each segment until you have teased out its full meaning.

10. **Put all the dream segments and their meanings together. Try to see what picture emerges and how each segment relates to the other ones.**

   After you understand what each segment means, assemble them all together so that you can see the whole picture. Look at how each segment relates to the other segments. This should allow you to determine what the whole dream is telling you.

   Once you know the meanings of your dream, you should have a feeling of resolution about the dream or a feeling that it feels more complete, as well as feeling some aha moments of recognition as the meanings resonate with you.

11. **Ask yourself what could have triggered your dream. Was it something you experienced during that day or the day before?**

   Knowing what might have triggered the dream can provide even more useful insight into its source, meanings, and what you may need to do with the information.

12. **Once you know the meanings of your dream, allow yourself to determine whether you need to work with the dream in any way.**

   Remember that you want to understand your dreams to use as a tool in your life. Once you understand what your dream is telling you, you'll want to figure out what to do with this information and how to apply and use it.

———

Next we'll look at some examples of each type of dream and what they might mean.

six

Dream Samples
and Their Interpretations

L et's look at some sample dreams and their interpretations. We'll explore them according to each type of dream. This will allow you to get a better sense of each type of dream, as well as a sense of how to interpret dreams. Some dream samples may be a combination of types but are put under the most prominent type that suits each dream. As you read each dream, try to get a sense of what it might mean.

Sorting Information,
Filing It Away, and Learning from It

Dream #1

I was being held prisoner somewhere. Every day a prison guard would make me leave my cell and take me up a long and steep ramp to a large room with no windows and a ceiling so high I couldn't see it. There were piles of things everywhere and a long conveyer belt. I had to stand at the conveyer belt and pack things into boxes. I couldn't see the boxes at first. They just seemed to appear out of thin air. No matter how many I packed, there were still more on the conveyer belt, which never stopped.

What do you make of this dream? There are certain elements of it that stand out, including a prison, a long and steep ramp, a high ceiling, no windows, a conveyer belt that never stopped, piles of things, and boxes. Clearly the dreamer feels constrained in this dream, but the dream could be referring to a number of possible situations.

In a situation like this, don't forget to dialogue with the dreamer. When I asked her if there was a situation in her life that felt constraining, if she had too much work to get done, and/or had a lot of piles or boxes, she shared that she was in the process of packing up her belongings to move. The day before she had this dream, she had devoted even more time to packing and had felt very frustrated by how much there was for her to do. It felt overwhelming and as if the packing would be interminable. She said that she had indeed felt like a prisoner and that it felt like a steep uphill climb (which is what the ramp in her dream symbolized).

This dream was simply expressing what the dreamer had been doing and how she had been feeling before she had the dream and thus contained no information requiring her to follow up on her dream in any way.

Dream #2

I've been in a cooking class, and yesterday we were learning about different herbs and spices and which foods they go well with. Last night I remember dreaming over and over again about herbs and spices. I would pick up a bottle, read the label, open it, and smell the spice. I would then think of the different foods it would go well with. I could practically smell each spice in my dream. I must have had at least three dreams like this.

This is a perfect example of a dream that is sorting information the dreamer was exposed to during the day and filing it away. This dream is obviously literal rather than symbolic and really requires no interpretation, as there is no emotionally flavored content. The dreamer shared at the outset that she was in a cooking class and had just learned about various herbs and spices. Had she not shared that information, it would have been important to dialogue with her to determine whether the dream was literal or symbolic and which part of her life it pertained to.

A dream like this, which is simply sorting information and filing it away for learning purposes and which has no emotional content, usually requires no follow-up on the part of the dreamer.

Expression of Bodily Conditions
Dream #3

> *In 1997 I dreamed that my stomach had swelled up to the size of a beach ball. It was huge. Inside of it were little balls that looked like billiard balls with circles in the center.*
>
> *When I awakened, my stomach was normal and I wondered what on earth that was! Months later I started getting sick with parasites. When I went to the lab for testing, I noticed that pinned up on a bulletin board was a newspaper article on parasites and a photo of a parasite called "blastocystis hominis." It looked exactly like the billiard balls in my dream.*

This is a perfect example of a dream expressing something going in the body. It needs no interpretation, as it's literal, and it demonstrates the knowledge and awareness that can be expressed in our dreams, whether coming from communication from our body to our mind, from a guide, or from intuitive knowing.

What is even more fascinating about this dream is that the dreamer saw exactly what the parasites looked like in her dream and had that confirmed months later. So we could also say that this was a clairvoyant dream, given the dreamer's glimpse of the parasite's structure.

Dream #4

I had a strange dream last night that I haven't been able to shake. I was looking at a map with a curvy road in the center of it. Next thing I knew, I was in my car going somewhere up a turning and twisting road, which felt like the road on the map. Then all of a sudden the road would be gone, as if a section of it had eroded or been washed away. I would then find myself doing the same thing again, as if the dream had started over, and would come to the part of the road that was gone. This must have gone on five or six times. Then it was like I was lifted out in space and I looked down and saw that the road was really my spine. Huh?! Then I woke up.

At first this dream may seem symbolic until we get to the part where the dreamer is looking down at the road and sees that it's actually his spine. Even though the dreamer sees his spine as a road with part of it missing, does that mean that there's any significance to the dream?

This is another example of how helpful it can be to dialogue with a dreamer to get additional information. I asked the dreamer if he'd had any back problems and he said that he'd had pain in his back for about six weeks. This additional information would seem to confirm that this dream was giving him information about what was going on with his back—that there's a physical problem that he needs to have medically addressed.

This dream was obviously a significant one for the dreamer, as opposed to dreams that may be expressing something going on in the body that has no importance, such as a full bladder.

Message Dreams

Dream #5

I had a dream in which my manfriend (who is a year older than I) and I were holding hands in a field, and my sister was giving the thumbs-up, and my friends were giving the thumbs-up, and my late mom and dad appeared above me in a heavenly cloud and beamed their approval. After a moment, my mom said, "If I hadn't met your dad when I did, and this man had been alive then, I would have taken him!"

This is obviously a positive dream with a positive message, as it expresses that several people close to the dreamer showed and stated their approval of the person the dreamer is romantically involved with. It has the added feature of the dreamer's deceased parents appearing in the dream and visiting her, while expressing their approval.

A psychologist might say that all the people appearing in the dream represented aspects of the dreamer herself and/or that the dreamer questioned whether her love interest was right for her and needed the validation of the dream. I feel, however, that her deceased parents were visiting her in the dream in order to communicate their approval of the man. Dialogue with the dreamer revealed that she had previously been married and was divorced, in addition to having been in other unsuccessful relationships. Thus, this dream's message was even more important for her.

Dream #6

I just had to share a dream my husband had last night (and he was not aware that I had been pondering this thought). He told me about his dream this morning.

He said he was in a very large, cold room in an ancient building with stone pillars/columns.

Four men were standing dressed in white robes/ cloaks in front of him. The hoods on their robes did not cover their heads, but were resting on their shoulders. They were higher up, as one would imagine a king sitting at the top of steps leading to a higher elevation of the floor.

Some of the men had white hair and possibly a beard, and some were younger with sandy brown hair. My husband was there to plead for me, to save me. I was also there, but I wasn't allowed to speak.

This "council" had come to the decision that I had broken one of the laws in the sacred spiritual connection to my twin flame. It was strictly forbidden to try to influence the twin to "wake up" and remember. It was against free will and they repeatedly told my husband, "It is a cardinal sin." Influencing the twin could make them come not from spirit but from ego, and it would make the connection IMPURE. Twins have to understand it from Spirit or it will "destroy" both twins. I was to be stripped of my holiness, my gifts, and condemned (to death). My husband is not sure if they meant spiritual death or actual physical death as well.

The men were holding either wooden or metal staffs, which were silver in color and were inscribed with symbols and letters. At the very top it looked like there were carved animal heads, possibly a lion on one of them. They were all different. It did not look like it was Indian-related (totem pole).

As the men lifted their staffs/rods to dunk them in the floor, as if to finalize their decision, my husband kept pleading to save me. He said, "She didn't know. Please don't do this." They stopped and said, "Because you are asking and because it is you, we will give her one more chance."

He woke up.

This dream is obviously a spiritual dream. While it's set in a spiritual setting and has a spiritual theme, I'm not convinced that it's an awakening dream. Instead, it feels to me that it's more of a message dream, because an important message is being conveyed to the dreamer—a message many people would benefit from learning about.

It's interesting that the message was conveyed by her husband in his dream to Annelie Pelfrey, who then shared it with me (and who asked that her name be used); that is, it was her husband who had the dream and not she, even though the dream was about her and conveying a message to her.

The fact that the guides were higher up would seem to convey that they were either "higher" guides (more elevated) or more spiritually advanced ones. It's interesting that the setting was in a "cold" room, and the severity of the message and the threat of death would appear to mirror the coldness of the room. The ancient building that the dream was set in is a fairly commonplace setting of some spiritual dreams. Many spiritual dreams are set in ancient buildings or temples, possibly to signify "universal" and "ancient" truths.

The dreamer shared that she had indeed been trying to get her husband to wake up spiritually and have spiritual realizations. She was given a strong message by this dream, however, that this was inappropriate and that she needed to let her husband unfold, learn, and grow in his own way and in his own time. This is what "it" is referring to in her dream account when she shared, "Twins have to understand it from Spirit"—"it" being spiritual awareness and spiritual growth. It should be a noted that this is a common mistake that many people make as they learn new things and unfold, whether it is in a spiritual context of awakening and growing spiritually or some other context of learning new things. People can get so excited by the new things they are learning that they want to proselytize and get others close to them on the same wavelength or "get them with the program." It's very important to let others unfold and grow in their own ways, whether spiritually or personally, without trying to goad or control them.

The dreamer asked me if I had ever heard the term "council" used in a spiritual context. Indeed I have. Although it's rare, some spiritually oriented people are consciously aware of being connected to a spiritual council on another, higher spiritual level. (A council or counselor in a dream may not always be referring to this type of spiritual council, however. One can usually determine or intuit from the context of the dream whether the reference is to a spiritual council or a counselor in three-dimensional reality.)

This dream gave a clear message to Ms. Pelfrey, with the expectation that she would take the message and act upon it. She shared with me that she knew she had to stop trying to intervene in her husband's spiritual path and let him take responsibility for that himself.

Communication Dreams, Including Visitation
Dream #7

I was preparing something to smoke, as in a pipe, when my dad (now deceased), with a beaming smile, brought two ceremonial pipes and suggested we smoke them instead of what I was preparing. It felt as if the pipes he brought had already been prepared to be smoked.

This is a short dream, but it turned out to be quite meaningful for the dreamer.

It immediately felt to me as if the dreamer's father had actually visited with him in the dream. Given that the pipes in the dream were ceremonial ones, it felt to me as if there was a sense of celebration. When I ran that by the dreamer, it turned out that he had felt that his father had not approved of some of his prior choices in life and that there had been tension between the two of them.

This dream, then, would be significant because it would appear that his father is indicating that the disapproval was in the past and that he now approves of his son.

The dreamer further shared that a few days before he had this dream, he had passed a college entrance exam in order to enroll in a pre-calculus class. This was of particular significance with regard to his father because the dreamer had not done well in calculus when he had attended college years earlier and had dropped out. His father had worked hard to pay for the dreamer's college tuition and had disapproved of his son's decision.

So the dreamer taking and passing a college entrance exam in order to retake calculus represents a redoing of something that had created a rift with his father. His dream is hugely significant because his father is celebrating with him and even smoking a "peace pipe" with him.

This dream marked a milestone for the dreamer. It represents a communication dream, a visitation one, and one in which something actually took place on some level, where peace was made between the dreamer and his father. A positive shift occurred. This was quite a powerful and positive dream!

Dream #8

I would like to share a dream I had last night that felt more like a visitation. I've been really preoccupied with it all day. I went to visit my aunt's house. (She's crossed over and so is her husband. We were very close.) I really felt I was there. I could hear the sounds of her apartment and smell the food cooking. Her husband, my uncle, was watching TV and showing me what was on the screen. My aunt then fed me macaroni and cheese with chopped-up hot dogs. I remember thinking, "Mmm, comfort food." She said, "Eat your daily bread," but in Spanish, so it was the line from the Lord's Prayer. I ate so much, like I hadn't eaten in years. It was delicious. Then I asked about my mom, and my aunt said, "Your

> *mother has to go through a heavy rainstorm, but it's
> okay, we're here." Then the phone rang and I answered
> it. It was my mother, upset that she was soaked from the
> rainstorm. I was very worried, but my aunt just said,
> "It's okay." I woke up in the middle of the night feeling
> worried for my mom. I can't shake this dream.*

At first glance, we know that this dream represented a
visitation, as the dreamer shared, and that she was both visiting and communicating with her deceased aunt and uncle.
This dream was obviously a significant one for the dreamer,
as she stated that she couldn't shake the dream.

I felt that there were meanings embedded in her dream
that the dreamer was having difficulty grasping. Intuitively I
was getting a sense of some of these meanings, but I wanted
to dialogue with the dreamer to get more input and verify
what I was getting.

I asked her what had stood out for her in the dream, and
she replied that the food and the worry about her mother
had. She further shared that her mother lived close by, but
that they weren't close to each other emotionally. This information confirmed what I had intuited.

The dreamer had been going through a difficult time
and was in need of some support and comfort, and her
dream was giving her that, as well as additional information. Her aunt and uncle, with whom she had been close,
were letting her know that they were still there for her and
would provide her with comfort (both the comfort food and
"your daily bread"). This was like manna from heaven for the
dreamer, as she said that the food was delicious and that she

ate like she hadn't in years; i.e., she really needed the support and comfort.

After the dreamer asked about her mother in the dream, it was revealed to her that her mother herself had been going through a hard time (when her aunt told her that her mother "had to go through a heavy rainstorm"). What her mother had been dealing with may have been putting her (the mother) in a bad mood, given that in the dream her mother called upset because of how the rainstorm had affected her (she had gotten wet). This also let the dreamer know that her mother may have been harder to get along with due to the problems she was dealing with. The dreamer was then given the message that her aunt and uncle were there for her, even if her mother hadn't been.

These meanings resonated for the dreamer and moved her emotionally. So the messages this dream gave the dreamer were very moving and comforting for her at a time when she was down.

Expressing Fears and Desires

Dream #9

I was at work—the building was a bit different from the "real" building, but most of the co-workers were the same. I was doing some editing work (that's my job) when I was notified that I was being let go. I didn't understand why, because my work and performance reviews are good. I didn't get any details or explanations.

When I sought out upper management, the COO told me that I had some mental illness problems and needed to get healthy. I then sought out the CEO, who was difficult to corner, but he said they were doing this for my own good because I needed to get help. I was confused in the dream as to whether this was supposed to be a temporary leave or a permanent dismissal, and I kept trying to get an answer without success.

I eventually started packing up my belongings and learned that one of my co-workers would be taking over my position and my office, even though this person didn't know a thing about editing.

I was quite fearful because I'm a single mom with two kids in college and didn't know how I would be able to pay the bills without my job. I woke up feeling sad and afraid.

This is obviously a scary dream, and the dreamer indeed shared that she woke up "feeling sad and scared." Is it precognitive or, instead, expressing fears?

If the dream is precognitive, then the scenario in the dream and the details of it should be either congruent with reality or symbolic. One detail in the dream is glaringly illogical. Can you see which one it is?

It's the detail about a specific co-worker taking over the dreamer's job, even though the co-worker "didn't know a thing about editing." It's obviously highly unlikely that a business would replace a competent employee who does specialized work with someone who lacks those specialized skills. Another illogical detail turned out to be the dreamer being told that she had a mental illness, which is not the case in real life. A third detail in the dream was a clue that this dream wasn't precognitive—that the building in her dream was "a bit different from the 'real' building."

So it would appear that this dream is expressing an underlying fear the dreamer has about losing her job. The next step would be trying to determine what could be triggering this fear.

The dreamer shared some extra information that shed light on this. She had recently experienced two losses: a relationship had ended badly, and her father had suddenly gotten critically ill and passed away. The dreamer had been so upset at the relationship break-up that she had gone on antidepressants. The part of the dream that speaks of a mental illness being the grounds for her dismissal from work would seem to be indicating that she felt some guilt or shame in having to take the medication (and, in fact, the dreamer shared that she's been tapering the dosage, as she no longer needs it).

These two sudden, unexpected losses that took place fairly close together in time could have engendered an underlying unconscious fear of something happening out of the blue that would constitute another loss, and her guilt over having to take the anti-depressants could be compounding that fear. (She may be concerned that her depression might somehow cause her dismissal from work.) I asked the dreamer if that resonated or felt like it could have triggered this dream, and she concurred.

Having a dream like this can be very scary because we may worry that it's precognitive. However, as you can see, there are clues in the dream itself that it's not in keeping with logical reality and does indeed stem from a fear. This dream would appear to be expressing the dreamer's fear and calling her attention to it. This then allows the dreamer to consciously acknowledge that the losses she has sustained have left her feeling fearful and vulnerable, so she can then work on the fear in some way. Because this dream is expressing the dreamer's fear, it would appear to be coming from her unconscious.

When we experience a serious loss—and especially when we suffer more than one of them in a short period of time—we will go through a grieving process, which we then need to heal from. Losses occurring close together can also trigger fears about sustaining more losses. This dream is merely highlighting that and bringing it to the dreamer's attention.

Dream #10

Last night I had several negative dreams. I was going to be on air as the morning anchor, and I had a Jolly Rancher stuck to my front teeth. My boyfriend cheated on me. My client told me I was second choice and wasn't getting the deal.

This dreamer had three negative dreams in one night. Can you determine what these dreams are about, or would you need more information in order to do that?

Generally and broadly speaking, there are two or three possibilities with regard to what may have caused these dreams. They could, of course, be precognitive, foretelling negative events that will happen at some point in the future. They could also be expressing underlying fears that the dreamer has. It's also possible that these dreams, given that all three occurred on the same night, could be serving as a relief valve for underlying fears.

The dreamer volunteered that things had been going well for her in both her relationship and her career. So I initially asked the dreamer if she had a fear of things suddenly falling apart, or if, because things were indeed going well, there could be a fear that it all couldn't be maintained. The dreamer replied that she feels adept at making things succeed, but not necessarily at maintaining success. So the dreams could have been expressing this underlying fear.

Note also that there is a thread running through the three dreams of being first in some way, because in these dreams she is a news anchor (meaning the lead journalist), she's in a committed relationship where she should come first to her boyfriend, and she wasn't the first choice for her client. So these dreams may be expressing an additional underlying fear about either not being first (which could stem from an underlying self-esteem issue about not being good enough) or not knowing how to sustain a lead position.

The words "anchor" and "Jolly" also appear to stand out. The dreamer shared that she does tend to be jolly, and the word "anchor" could be evoking the sense of being able to anchor her success. In the first dream, having the Jolly Rancher stuck to her teeth would seem to imply something unforeseen marring her performance and/or that she isn't prepared to take the lead, both of which would again be fears.

I'm not convinced that these dreams are precognitive. Having all three of them in one night underscores the likelihood that they stem from underlying fears. Moreover, the possibility of these dreams expressing fears did resonate with the dreamer.

The good news is that the dreamer can take the realization she may have gleaned from these dreams about an underlying fear and work on it. EFT (Emotional Freedom Technique) would be an excellent modality to use, and there are other helpful healing modalities that could be used, which you'll find listed in appendix A.

It feels very likely to me that something the dreamer experienced the day she had these dreams or the day before could have triggered the underlying fears and that these dreams sprang from her unconscious. In this regard, her unconscious is aiding her on her journey to wholeness and balance. The dreamer can then partner with her unconscious by working on what it has revealed to her. Great stuff!

Creative Inspiration and Problem-Solving
Dream #11

I have VERY vivid, movie-like, detailed dreams. I have had dreams all my life where I am able to do things in detail that in my awake life I have either never experienced or don't know how to do. For instance, as a teenager, I would dream of entire cheerleading routines and then wake up and teach them to my squad. As an adult, I have dreamt of building an entire gazebo, piece by piece, nail by nail, in such detail that if I'd had the inkling, I could have built it in real life by myself.

Remember that we each have our own individual style of dreaming? Well, this dreamer's account of many of her dreams illustrates that. This dreamer is fortunate to have had many dreams that are creative and have shown her how to do different things. It's as if her dreams are not only showing her things, but also teaching her.

Dreaming of techniques that are instructing us on how to do things is a very special skill, although the dreamer may not have consciously tried to cultivate it. This account, however, shows us what is possible in dreams. This is a marvelous ability!

We don't know how the dreamer gets this knowledge in her dreams. She could be tapping into knowledge (or information) as energy or be given the information through guides or passed-on loved ones. It would be nice to know how she's getting the information and knowledge and what the source is. However, the striking takeaway from these dreams is that receiving information and knowledge we didn't have is definitely a possibility in our dreams.

You might want to try incubating dreams like this yourself!

Dream #12

To improve the efficiency of my vehicle's engine, I was shown how to reduce a frequency or a rate (not sure which) by using a meter of some type that resembled a wand with a digital display on one end of it. I believe the adjustment had something to do with the ignition system, and the amount of reduction was by a factor of four. In the back of the manual for this procedure was also the instruction to replace the engine oil with an old off-brand of oil. As I recall, the first letter of the brand started with the letter K ("Kent," maybe).

This is an interesting, if also somewhat technical, dream. I felt that this was a very creative dream, in that the dreamer might have been given useful information, enabling him to do some problem-solving. I asked the dreamer if he had indeed been chewing in real life on a way to improve the efficiency of his vehicle, and he shared that he had, because he had been getting very poor gas mileage. Initially the dreamer hadn't realized that this dream was giving him an answer, because the vehicle in his dream was different from the one he was driving in real life. Upon reflection, he realized that it was a possible solution and said that he was going to check it out with a dealership.

So it would appear that this is a creative problem-solving dream, in which the dreamer was given a solution to his problem. You'll note that the details in the dream are very technical ones. However, the dreamer himself has a technical background, so the technical nature of his dream didn't feel entirely foreign to him.

This is a fairly short dream, but it's an excellent example of a creative problem-solving dream in which a solution to a problem we have been facing is given to us in the dream state. This further illustrates how we can be given useful information and answers to problems in our dreams. We can work on incubating dreams like this to increase the likelihood of receiving helpful information. The information in this dream could have come from the dreamer's unconscious, a guide, or even someone else (including a passed-on loved one). It would certainly be worth following up on!

Expressing Personal Issues and Personal Process, and Working Issues Out

Dream #13

A street fair was happening just outside my door, with wandering minstrels, jesters carrying cameras, lovers in open windows, Maypole dancers, etc. I was frantically searching for the fan deck, while my sister was outside the door, tapping her foot impatiently, arms folded, and muttering, "Can't you keep track of anything?"

My body walked around, while my head lay on the pillow, barking orders. Various items of antique furniture materialized, and my arms looked through each one, while the jesters danced lightly among the open drawers. I was hoping that I could gather some money so I could buy some things, but whenever my hands encountered coins, etc., the coins would drop through my hands like they weren't there, and jingle noisily on the floor. Finally, in a pot-bellied chest of drawers, the fan deck was discovered in the bottom drawer, wrapped in a tan grocery bag. Just as my body screwed my head on and handed the fan deck to my sister and the furniture melted away, I woke up.

This dream is rich with intriguing imagery and symbols. Can you get a sense of what this dream is indicating?

This is another excellent example of a dream in which dialoguing with the person who had the dream yielded additional information and insight. The dreamer added the following statement, giving some background on a real-life situation that had preceded her dream: "Back in December,

I moved into a new house (well, new to me). My sister lent me her paint color fan deck (a thick book of paint color samples, used by professional painters). Since then, there's been a lot of upheaval, and the fan deck has vanished, possibly into the hoarder's dream that is my car. My sister asked for it last night, to be produced immediately, if not sooner."

This dream expresses differences in personal characteristics between her sister and her that lead the dreamer to feel inadequate and down on herself. Her sister is clearly upset over the dreamer's inability to keep track of the item she lent her. The dreamer feels that she is irresponsible in her life, while her sister is the responsible one, which is expressed in this dream.

The dream expresses the dreamer's preference for play and creativity (participating in the street fair, being among the vivid colors) rather than taking care of mundane responsibilities. The dream is also expressing the dreamer's negative self-talk, that she "couldn't find her head unless it's screwed on to her body," a colloquial expression referring to the inability to be responsible and rational. (This is conveyed in the dream by her head lying on the pillow, barking orders, while her body walked around.)

The dream further expresses negative self-talk about the dreamer being bad with money, through the image of the coins continually falling through her fingers, representing her inability to hold on to money. This part of the dream is visually expressing the idiomatic expression "Money just slips through his fingers."

Additional symbols that stand out as potentially significant include the antique furniture, the pot-bellied chest of drawers, and the "jesters" that "danced lightly among the open drawers." Do you have a sense of what they could signify?

The antique furniture ended up signifying that this was an old issue that figuratively serves as furniture or furnishings in her mind (self-image), and the pot-bellied chest of drawers referred to the dreamer's image of herself as pot-bellied in some way, or, because the fan deck was found there, it may simply symbolize her responsibility or culpability for misplacing the color fan deck there. It may be meaningful that the fan deck was found in this chest of drawers "wrapped in a tan grocery bag." The tan grocery bag is plain, in stark contrast to all the implied colors of the street fair, which may signify that the dreamer prefers the colorfulness of artistic and fun endeavors more than the everyday and drab. The jesters dancing lightly among the open drawers would appear to signify that, as the dreamer kept looking for the fan deck, the pull of the street fair (symbolized by the jesters) kept pulling at her, as she preferred to attend the street fair. They could also be evoking the sense that her sister's view of her as irresponsible kept taunting her, even if in jest.

This is obviously a dream that expresses personal issues and one in which it would appear that the dreamer's unconscious is expressing a lack of inner harmony because of her negative self-image. In other words, the dreamer's negative self-image and negative self-talk keep her from feeling whole and content within herself, and this disparity is being expressed by her unconscious in the dream, especially in contrast with her sister. In spite of the fact that the dreamer is quite accomplished in many ways, this dream shows that she doesn't see herself as such.

The dream could have the purpose of bringing these underlying issues to light and more conscious awareness. The dreamer could take the information gleaned from the dream and work with it for self-healing via a healing modality. You'll find a list of healing modalities in appendix A.

I feel that this is an excellent example of a dream that is rich with symbolism expressing inner issues that could then be worked on in a move toward healing and greater wholeness.

Dream #14—First Dream

I dreamed that I was at a basement party. It was the 1970s, so there were lots of people walking around in jeans and long hair. There were also quite a few sofas in the basement. I could see a big-screen TV at the end of the basement, but nothing was playing on it. Mom was dressed nicely, in a white sweater and brown plaid slacks, but I had to prop her up against a column in the basement. She was asleep and was unaware of what was going on, but she kept peeing. The pee never affected her clothing but instead just created a puddle on the floor. All I could do was prop her up against a column at the party and keep cleaning up after her. I walked down the hall to wash my hands, and there was a door going to the outside. The sign above it said "Door of Past Regrets." I chose not to go through that door, but instead walked into the restroom and washed my hands. When I went back, Mom was still propped up against the wall, and I had to clean up the floor yet again.

When I woke up, I asked for clarification on the dream because it was so real. So I had another dream.

Dream #14—Second Dream

I dreamed that I was in a river. The shore was not so far away, but it was partially frozen, as if a glacier had broken, and there were lots of blocks of ice, slush, and frozen debris in the river. The shore was not far from me, and there appeared to be about twelve inches between the top of the shore and the water. While the river was not cold, it was hard to swim in because of all of the ice debris.

I was swimming along, and behind me and further in the river was my sister, who was swimming about thirty yards behind me but out in the middle of the river. And about thirty yards behind her was another figure swimming who was further out in the middle of the river. That figure seemed to be my niece, but she was not as clear.

When I went to get out of the river, the shore morphed to a cliff-sized shore, maybe fifty feet high, and I was climbing up, hanging on to icy brackets stuck in the wall. Behind me was my sister trying to climb out as well. I was about three-quarters of the way up the cliff and my sister was in the lower one-quarter crawling out. My niece was still far out in the river swimming.

I understood that we had gotten in this river and thought it would be easy to get out. Instead, it was extraordinarily difficult to climb out of this river.

These dreams are full of information for the dreamer and, to me, have to do with issues the dreamer had had with her mother.

The setting of the first dream in a basement stands out as significant. We often think of our personal issues lying deeper in our psyches—in the "basement" of our consciousness. The fact that this party was taking place in the 1970s would seem to mean that that time period was one in which the dreamer's mother had more influence over her that related to the unresolved issues. The details of a party, several sofas, and a TV would seem to imply leisure (even if the big-screen TV was anachronistic for the 1970s). However, the dreamer can't rest or socialize in the dream, so there's a contrast between the leisure/socializing details in the dream and the dreamer's need to attend to her mother. In addition, "nothing…playing" on the TV also seems to reflect that the dreamer isn't playing.

Even though her mother is dressed nicely, she's asleep and needs to be propped up. The mother being propped up may refer to the dreamer feeling on some level that she had to "prop her mother up" in life, while her mother's being asleep could mean that her mother wasn't aware or was oblivious to what was going on around her and/or that her mother wasn't aware spiritually.

As you might guess, the details of her mother repeatedly urinating and the dreamer needing to clean up are meaningful ones. It's significant that the urine doesn't get on her mother's clothing and pools on the floor. This, to me, may signify that her mother's presentation of herself to the world is that she is together and well-dressed but that she is soiling other things around her inappropriately, creating quite a contrast between her social persona and her personal or private habits. Furthermore, in this context the detail that she "was asleep and was unaware of what was going on" would seem to underscore that the mother was not only unaware of but oblivious to some of the things she did that affected others and that required others around her to take care of or clean up after her.

Another possible meaning of the dreamer's mother repeatedly urinating may signify her being full of toxic substances that need to be excreted or that she "unloads" inappropriately—or both. She may express her feelings or judgments fairly consistently in a way that is toxic. The dreamer, her daughter, needs to attend to her mother instead of being able to enjoy herself at this party and also has to clean up after her.

The detail of the door marked "Door of Past Regrets" that leads to the outside, when she leaves the room to wash her hands, is significant as well. To me, the door represents the possibility of the dreamer holding on to regrets about her mother. Significantly, the dreamer chooses not to go out that door to the outside and instead opts to simply wash her hands and then dutifully return to taking care of her mother and cleaning up after her. This implies that the dreamer didn't waste her energy in regrets, but instead continued to clean up after her mother and care for her.

Dialogue with the dreamer yielded even more information. She acknowledged major and long-lasting issues with her mother, who tended to hamper her in her life. So this dream is expressing those issues and the fact that they still reside within her (in the "basement" of her consciousness). In her dream, the dreamer was dutiful in cleaning up after her mother and attending to her needs, but was prevented from relaxing and enjoying herself as a result. Nonetheless, she continued to attend to her mother and be the obedient child and didn't hold on to regrets.

In the second dream, which should provide clarifying information for her, she finds herself figuratively swimming upstream among ice and icy debris. Both her sister and her niece are also in this icy river, trying to navigate it, with her niece the farthest behind and in the middle of the river. The dreamer, significantly, is in the lead and ahead of her sister and niece.

It would appear that this dream may be expressing that all three of the people in it are trying to move forward in life, having been affected by the dreamer's mother and possibly other relatives, including the dreamer's niece's family. The dreamer is the furthest along in moving forward and perhaps also in resolving or no longer being affected by her issues with family. Her niece may be trying to take the middle ground in life, since she is in the middle of the river.

It's noteworthy that, even with all the ice, the river isn't cold. It's still hard to navigate, however, because of all the ice. It feels to me that the river may be a metaphor for the "river of life" that all three of them are trying to move through. It's significant that the dreamer shared that the river "was hard to swim in because of all of the ice debris." Given the dreamer's mother continually urinating in the first dream, it feels that the "ice debris" in the second dream may symbolize all the frozen, almost ossified "debris" or remnants (or lasting effects) of her mother's toxic unloading. In other words, the urine from the first dream has crystallized and turned into icy debris in the dreamer's adult life and made it difficult for her to move through life easily. It's possible that the iciness could also be alluding to her mother having been "icy" or less than warm. However, the dreamer is either doing better than her sister and niece or is leading them, as in the second dream she is ahead of them in the river (of life).

Even after she gets out of the river, the dreamer is faced with a difficult and still icy climb up the cliff. There are icy brackets in the wall of the cliff to hold on to, but the dreamer still has to climb up herself. The fact that the icy brackets are there may represent help being given to her from someone or from guides in her arduous climb up and away from the effects of her upbringing. The icy brackets could also be signifying some other remnant of her mother's influence on her that may be helpful to her in her climb. The fact that she was three-quarters of the way up the cliff may be expressing that the dreamer is three-quarters of the way through working out and resolving her issues around her mother, and the fact that the cliff is about "fifty" feet tall could signify something significant for the dreamer around the age of fifty.

To me, this is a hugely significant dream for the dreamer. It is showing her how she was affected by her mother, that those issues still reside in the deeper levels of her consciousness. She has elected not to just walk away from (or deny the existence of) those issues and regret them, but instead to work on them. She is making progress, even if somewhat tortuously, toward healing from the issues.

It feels as if this dream has sprung from the dreamer's unconscious and is expressing where the dreamer is with regard to healing the issues from her childhood. The last part of the second dream, with the dreamer leaving the river and slowly climbing up the cliff, could represent encouragement to her and assurance from her unconscious that she is indeed making progress and healing.

This dream is an excellent example of this type of dream and how much information we can derive from such a dream. It should serve as encouragement to the dreamer for all her ongoing work in working on these issues. She's definitely being told that she's making strong progress.

Healing Dreams

Dream #15

I dreamt that I was in the living room of a house. I was looking out the picture window and knew that the house across the street was J's house. As I looked, two moving vans pulled up from the left. The vans left and J came out of the house. He stood in the middle of the street and turned to look straight into my house. It seemed that he looked into my eyes, but I knew he shouldn't be able to see me inside. He had a sadness in his eyes with an apology and a goodbye look. I knew he was indicating that he really did care and was sorry. A helicopter then arrived, from the right, and he climbed in and it flew away.

This is a very interesting dream and it actually contains a hint as to its meaning: "I knew that he was indicating that he really did care and was sorry."

This is an excellent example of a healing dream. It did require dialoguing with the dreamer to get the full meanings of it, though, as it wasn't straightforward or literal.

The dreamer shared that she had been able to incubate several healing dreams before this one, simply by asking before going to sleep that she be given a healing dream. Indeed, she had asked for a healing dream on the night that she had this dream.

This dream pertained to a relationship she had been in that had ended somewhat badly two years prior to her having this dream. She had terminated the relationship, feeling that the guy really didn't care for her. Since that time, she had been somewhat wracked by hurt feelings, and she felt that this dream actually gave her a healing from all of the pain and remorse.

So what are the indications in this dream of information that helped to resolve and heal her negative and hurt feelings?

In the dream, she was in her house and he was in the house directly across the street. When she orally recounted the dream, there was an emphasis on the phrase "*my* house" that leapt out at me. This, to me, indicated that she was very much into where she was at the time with regard to her mindset and feelings, which is predicated upon the house in her dream signifying her mind or "where she lived," figuratively speaking (a meaning that we've covered before). The fact that she was looking out of a large picture window would seem to imply that she had a good, large, and/or expansive view from her vantage point and was an open person and also possibly vulnerable.

It's significant that their houses were directly across the street from each other. This, to me, was signifying that they were at different places in their lives, and that their minds, attitudes, or ways of seeing things were somewhat opposed. In other words, they weren't coming from the same place.

Two moving vans came to his house from the left. It's significant that the moving vans came from the "left." This could be a play on words, indicating that the man would be gone because he would have "left." It's also meaningful that he came to the middle of the street when he turned and looked at her house. That may be implying that his attitude, stance, or mindset had changed and he had moved midway toward her mindset or outlook. It also implied that he had moved closer to her. His looking at her with sadness, an apologetic look, and a seeming goodbye were implying that he regretted what had happened between the two of them and that he really had cared about her. Nonetheless, he was moving on with his life, which was signified by the moving vans.

It's interesting that a helicopter arrived and that that was his means of departure. This is an unusual detail. I asked the dreamer what she thinks of when she thinks of helicopters, and she stated that she thinks of rescue ones. So the detail of his leaving on a helicopter implies rescue, whether she was the one being rescued by his departure (or by her having this dream) or he was. Of course, it could imply that the healing quality of this dream was healing for both of them, with the end result of both of them being "rescued" by the dream taking place. The fact that the helicopter came from the right may signify that this was the "right" thing to happen.

The fact that the dreamer had incubated the dream and, indeed, had had several healing dreams prior to this one shows that one can learn to incubate dreams and that healing dreams are possible and helpful. Being able to incubate healing dreams can be a hugely beneficial tool for personal and spiritual growth and unfolding. This dreamer is obviously quite adept at it.

The dreamer said that this dream enabled her to move past the hurt feelings and resolve what had happened, so she didn't necessarily need to follow through with any action. The dream itself resolved an issue for her and is a wonderful example of a healing dream. This dream likely came from her unconscious, or possibly a guide, or both.

When we have a healing dream, whether we incubated it or not, we feel better and are able to resolve an issue or begin to do so, because the dream itself triggers a healing. When we actually incubate a healing dream, we are partnering with the universe or our unconscious in our process of unfolding and growing.

Dream #16

I had this dream on the morning of New Year's Eve. I was in a town near my childhood home with my older sister. We were outside in freshly fallen snow and it was continuing to fall from the sky. There were no tracks of any kind in the snow. It was a glorious sight and it felt wonderful to be there. We saw a woman who beaconed [sic] us to come with her, which we did. As we walked along, she began to sing Christmas carols and we joined in. Soon others were coming out of their homes and singing with us. The feeling was truly blissful. We came to a '65 Mustang and the woman invited us to go with her. Another woman joined us, and my sister and I were climbing into the back seat, but I got wedged and had great difficulty getting in (I am a large woman) but finally did. When I was finally in the back seat, I found that it was really quite spacious, just the getting-in part was difficult.

After we had been traveling in this car a relatively short time, I looked up front and found that the dashboard actually had a stairway going down, and I could see the woman whom I believed to be driving downstairs. It looked so inviting and I wanted to join her. As I went down the stairs, I found that it was a wonderful place, warm and inviting, with a fireplace and lots of sunlight (interesting for a basement). As I basked in the warmth of this "basement," a man appeared and there was great tenderness and caring between the woman and man. When the man stepped away for a moment, I asked the woman if that was her husband. She replied that he wasn't. He wanted to marry her, but she wasn't ready yet. The time was not right.

This is a very interesting dream with several significant symbols in it, including New Year's Eve, childhood home, sister, freshly fallen snow, no tracks in the snow, the woman, singing Christmas carols, '65 Mustang, back seat, getting wedged in the seat, spacious, stairway going down, lots of sunlight in the basement, man, and great tenderness and caring. Can you get a sense of what any of these symbols may mean?

I initially got several impressions from this dream. The fact that the dreamer had this dream on the morning of New Year's Eve, to me, signifies new beginnings, as it's right on the cusp of a new year. The setting of the dreamer's childhood home with her sister present in the dream would seem to imply that the dream may have had to do with family in some way and/or memories or issues that stem from childhood. The freshly fallen snow with no tracks also conveys a sense of newness and freshness, and the dreamer felt good being there. The woman feels to me as if she were a guide for the dreamer. The fact that the woman "beaconed" the dreamer, instead of "beckoned" her, feels to me like a meaningful Freudian slip, as it conveys the sense that the woman was a beacon (of light), further underscoring her being a guide. There's a sense of a positive feeling connected with being with others, as connoted by singing Christmas carols with others and the blissful feeling.

The '65 Mustang may be indicating that the year 1965 was significant in some way and may be connected to the setting in the dream. The dreamer being concerned about not fitting into the car and then finding that it was spacious may be signifying that the dreamer holds herself back over concern about herself, whether her weight or other negative judgments, and has difficulty trying new things, but that she actually fits in well.

The fact that her sister and she were in the back seat is also significant and may indicate that the dreamer is allowing her guide (the woman) to lead her.

Going down the stairway to a lower or deeper level is also meaningful. It may be pointing to going to deeper levels, possibly of consciousness. The fact that there was lots of sunlight there may be conveying that when she goes deeper, there is light, both illumination and positive energy.

In actuality, dialogue with the dreamer yielded even more insight. It turned out that 1965 was a very significant year for her, because that was the year her father had open-heart surgery, and he was one of the first patients to have that kind of surgery. He was hospitalized from October to the following May, and the dreamer recalled feeling very scared about how her father was doing during his surgery.

The dreamer initially felt that the newly fallen snow represented "a kind of uncharted territory" for her to travel. This parallels her father's surgery, since he was one of the first people to have open-heart surgery. Given the dreamer's fear of getting wedged while trying to get into the car, which may have signified a fear of trying new things, the dream may be indicating that her fears started with her father's surgery (since he was one of the first ones to try open-heart surgery and she felt such fear at the time). This may also explain why the dreamer's sister was with her in the back seat, forming the connection with the year 1965 and her father.

The fact that the dreamer was able to get into the car and found it to be more spacious, after she had initially feared it wouldn't be, would seem to be telling her that it was okay to try new things and that she would find that they were easier than she had anticipated (since the car turned out to be more spacious).

By the dreamer getting into the back seat of the car and allowing the woman (who signified her guide) to drive, the dreamer is allowing her guide to lead her in life. In fact, the dreamer discovers a stairway after a short period of time and feels comfortable in following her guide down it. The dreamer herself shared that "going downstairs indicated that the path with my higher self/guide was going to require me to go deeper" and that if she stayed in the car—i.e., on a more superficial level—she would be separated from her guide or higher self. She wanted more information in the dream, but her phone rang and woke her.

The dream appears to be indicating to the dreamer that her fear of trying new things—which started with the fear associated with her father trying a new thing (open-heart surgery)—can now be worked on and healed through her spiritual orientation and letting her guide lead her deeper, and that this is the way to heal that fear.

In the dream, she found that the deeper level was beautiful, with warmth, lots of sunlight (signifying illumination and positive energy), and the caring man there. I feel that the man in that part of the dream is indicating that she will meet a very caring man through her work of going deeper, even though the time (at the time of the dream) wasn't quite right.

This is a very rich dream from the standpoint of the extent of the meanings for the dreamer. It's a healing one, because it's giving the dreamer information on how to heal the fears she's held since her youth, and also a spiritual one that contains important messages for the dreamer. This dream may be stemming from the dreamer's unconscious, a guide, and/or her higher soul awareness.

The knowledge of how to follow up on the dream is contained within the dream itself, and the dreamer indicated that she was determined to be on the spiritual path that would lead her deeper.

Psychic Dreams, Including Precognition, Clairvoyance, etc.

Dream #17

I dreamed a few weeks ago that I was riding in the car and the "sun" was shooting down to Earth at a distance behind us ... but it was still normal daylight. I don't know how long that worried me. But was it the sun or was it the meteor?

At first glance, this seems to be a provocative dream and could have been literal or symbolic. Could it have been apocalyptic, perhaps triggered by all the talk about being in "end times" or about climate change?

As it turned out, this dream was literal. However, the person who had this dream didn't realize what it was about until February 15, 2013. That was the day a meteor entered the earth's atmosphere and exploded into pieces in the air above the town of Chelyabinsk in Russia. When the dreamer heard about the meteor in Russia, he realized that that was what his dream had been about. He shared the following:

I just saw a video clip where someone was filming the meteor in Russia while they were going down the road … and it was shining like the sun as it hit the atmosphere. It reminded me of the dream.

This is an excellent example of a precognitive dream. Some people may feel that when you have a dream that's precognitive, you will know what it's about and what it's foretelling. This is not always true, as exemplified by this dream. It's only after the event happens that we realize what our dream was about and that it was precognitive, especially if we have a feeling of resolution after the event occurs. If we don't feel that the dream's ambiguity is resolved, then we may still not know what the dream was about and whether it was precognitive.

With a dream like this, there's little we need to do after having had it, aside from being watchful to see what, if anything, occurs. Since this dream was precognitive, it lets the dreamer know that he has intuitive ability, whether he has claimed and developed this potential or not.

As a result of having this dream, the dreamer could indeed follow up by developing his latent intuitive ability.

Dream #18

A few months ago, I dreamed that my oldest brother [who was in waking reality being treated for cancer] was going to go to the hospital the next day. In the dream, I saw him sweating a great deal, and also saw him perk up when his grandkids came to visit him in his room. I was aware that when he went to the hospital, he would be in contact with our mother, as if she were at the same hospital [though she actually passed away a few years back]. I left his room when he got too tired for our visit, though I joked that I was more comfortable sitting with him and leaning on him.

This dream, to me, has a very clear message. What do you get out of it?

The dreamer shared that in real life her brother does have cancer and is undergoing treatment for it. In her dream, he goes into the hospital the next day. The next part of her dream feels as if she is clairvoyantly watching him while he is in the hospital, because she can see him sweating and interacting with his grandchildren. So this part of the dream feels to me as if it's not symbolic, but is instead a clairvoyant observation, even though it occurs on the next day (in the future). In this part of the dream, a part of her consciousness may actually have gone to the future where she was observing her brother—or it's also possible that she was being shown this scene by a guide or other being, even a passed-on loved one.

The next part of the dream feels to me as if it's the most significant—"I was aware that when he went to the hospital, he would be in contact with our mother, as if she were at the same hospital."

The dreamer shared that in reality her mother was deceased. So this part of the dream would appear to be giving the dreamer the message that her brother won't make it and will instead pass away, because her brother "will be in contact" with their deceased mother.

The dreamer shared that her brother did indeed have to be admitted to the hospital the day after she had this dream. Furthermore, he did have "profuse sweating," and he did indeed "perk up" whenever his grandchildren were visiting him there. And he didn't make it. A few days later, he did indeed pass away.

So this dream turned out to be precognitive as well as clairvoyant, and it was actually preparing the dreamer on some level for her brother's passing, even if she didn't know at the time she had the dream whether it was a fictitious scenario or truly precognitive. The precognitive part of the dream was subtle enough in referring simply to "contact," however, so that the information about her brother passing wouldn't be too blatant. It would appear that the dreamer was close to her brother, given the last part of the dream in which she joked that she "was more comfortable sitting with him and leaning on him." If this is true, having a little bit of a heads-up that his passing was imminent could have helped to prepare her emotionally for his death.

So this dream would appear to be a gift that she was given and represents an intuitive insight that helped to prepare her for what was going to happen to a loved one of hers.

Actual Experiences and Exploring, Including Past-Life Memories

Dream #19

When I was little, I would have a dream that would come back to me over and over. It was one of seeing big mushroom clouds and then seeing a wall of light, then feeling hot, then nothing, just numb. The dreams that

would come later were of looking outside and the sky
and everything had a red tint to it, and people had to
wear a crazy space-looking suit to go outside.

In spite of this being a recurring dream, the fact that the dreamer had these dreams when he was little feels quite significant. You'll note the detail of the "big mushroom clouds." Obviously those are the mark of a nuclear bomb detonation.

There are various possibilities as to what this dream could be about. Given the fact that these dreams began in the dreamer's childhood, there's a possibility that he either saw a film about a nuclear bomb and its aftermath or heard family members, a teacher, or someone else he knew discussing how devastating a nuclear bomb could be and how it could kill off life, both people and animals. If this were the case, it would make perfect sense that the dreamer could have recurring dreams expressing an underlying fear of going through such a terrible disaster. It's also possible that something in the dreamer's life triggered the underlying fear.

A second possibility is that these dreams were precognitive and that the dreamer was dreaming about nuclear bomb detonations that may happen in the future—whether he is actually in the location where a nuclear bomb is detonated, is affected by a nuclear bomb disaster, or knows people who will be affected by such an awful event. The persistence of the recurring dreams, to me, implies some sort of emotional charge to these dreams, meaning that he may be directly affected in some way or that there is a greater likelihood of the event occurring and his being affected when it does.

A third possibility is that these recurring dreams were actually from a past-life experience in which he was indeed affected by a nuclear-bomb detonation. Of course, the ones that come to mind were those of the nuclear bombs dropped on Hiroshima and Nagasaki in World War II (which helped to end that terrible global war). If the dreamer had actually lived in one of those cities when the nuclear bombs were dropped, that could have caused these recurring dreams. (Recurring dreams that occur and recur during childhood about an event or place far away from where the child lives frequently stem from an unconscious past-life memory that may not yet have been completely resolved.)

I personally tend to lean toward the third possibility, that of these dreams stemming from a past life of the dreamer. You'll note that the dream account appears to be a firsthand account, as if the event were being recalled. Consider the part in which he wrote of "seeing big mushroom clouds and then seeing a wall of light, then feeling hot, then nothing, just numb." How would a child know that if a nuclear bomb went off, you would see a wall of light, then feel hot, and then go numb? This to me has the feel of a memory of something that was actually experienced. Yes, a child could imagine this effect or may have observed it in a film, but that feels less likely to me.

If these recurring dreams do stem from a past life of the dreamer in which he lived in either Nagasaki or Hiroshima when the nuclear bombs were dropped, the fear surrounding the past-life experience could have engendered an underlying fear of it happening again (because the emotions, trauma, or awareness of past experiences, when strong enough, can be carried in our unconscious).

Past-life regression could enable the dreamer to determine if he did indeed go through an atomic-bomb detonation in World War II and then begin to resolve any residual issues from the trauma of that experience. This could possibly and hopefully lead to quelling any fears about it happening again.

Remember that our unconscious is trying to bring us to balance and wholeness, because it's our inner ally. For this reason, I don't feel that bad dreams and nightmares are a plague or an attempt on the part of the unconscious to either punish us or make us miserable. Instead, I feel that nightmares represent an attempt on the part of our unconscious to let us know where there is an imbalance and what it would be helpful for us to work on in ourselves for our unfolding and betterment—truly to help restore us to balance and wholeness and thus greater happiness.

Dream #20

I dreamed I was in my bedroom (that I shared with my husband, who was then working the night shift), and in our bed. There was a glow coming through the window from the yard behind my apartment. I went outside in my PJs and walked around the apartment to the backyard area. There was a disk-shaped spaceship parked there, with a staircase coming out the bottom of it (just like in the movies). I was not afraid. In fact, I was compelled to climb the stairs. When I got to the top, an alien (also like in the movies…large head, large eyes…lack of defined features…pale in color) starting communicating with me telepathically. He explained that I was to enter the craft and take a seat. He (it) said I would be taken on a tour of the universe, and that my reaction to the sights I would see would be monitored and measured. I was told that I was being invited on this tour as part of an effort to determine if humans on Earth were ready to know of their existence.

I entered the craft. There were two rows of seats with an aisle between them, and two seats on each side of the craft, like an airplane. I took a seat near a window. We picked up a few more people, then we went on a tour. There were other people on the craft, but I didn't focus much on them. We were whisked off to strange places. In the dream, I remembered them showing me colors that I had never seen before. (When I woke up, I couldn't remember what they looked like because I had no frame of reference for them, but in the dream I was exhilarated to know there were other colors beyond anything we've ever seen.) I saw "buildings" that were spiral-shaped and seemed to be built in the middle of space—not attached to anything resembling a planet—and the significance of the shape was explained to me (although I didn't remember the significance when I woke up).

Then we started delivering people back to their homes. When it was my turn to "de-craft," I was told telepathically that my cooperation was appreciated and that I should return to my bed. I was also told that when I woke up, I would be fully rested, and I would think this had all been a dream.

This is quite a dream, isn't it? The dreamer added, "I distinctly remember checking to see if I had grass clippings or moisture on my feet when I woke up. I was SURE it had really happened. This dream took place about thirty-five years ago, and to this day I remember it in as much detail as I did the next morning."

The dreamer feels that this was an actual experience rather than something she had dreamed about. We might typically feel that this was a UFO abduction, as there are many reports of people having them during the night. I'm not convinced, though, that this is what it was. There are two details in this "dream" that, to me, don't feel congruent with a true UFO abduction. First of all, the spaceship in this account was just like the ones seen in movies. This, to me, is more like the suggestion of a UFO, but isn't a real one. It's too much like a Hollywood depiction. Secondly, the ETs seen were also seemingly straight out of Hollywood: "an alien (also like in the movies…large head, large eyes…lack of defined features…pale in color)." It's as if the dreamer is supposed to feel that it's a UFO abduction because of the movie-like depictions.

Additionally, the detail of the colors that the dreamer sees would be more evocative of a near-death experience (NDE) than a UFO abduction. Various people who have had an NDE have reported seeing beautiful colors unlike anything seen on Earth. So the colors that the dreamer sees don't feel to me like a UFO abduction.

The detail of the "spiral-shaped" buildings is an interesting one, given that the dreamer saw them in space unattached to anything. She shared with me that "the spiral buildings were the things that really confused me, because they were not attached to any form of planet, just hovering in space, and defied the laws of physics as I experience them on Earth. I did feel like they were tangible buildings, however."

The dreamer was guided throughout this experience—in my view, not by an ET, but instead by a guide. And she had other human companions on this journey. So it was made more real by the human company she had.

The dreamer felt that this was an actual experience, and her recall of it, as she stated, is unchanged since that evening over thirty-five years ago. She could have been taken on a tour of our three-dimensional cosmos, or to another dimension, or possibly to a higher vibrational level or the "other side."

I feel that this was an actual experience—a spiritual one—for the dreamer. She shared that she had had a near-death experience when she was nine months old, and this "dream" experience may have further triggered or opened her spiritually. She shared that she often views the two experiences as connected, which makes perfect sense, especially if they are serving as spiritual-opening experiences, as I feel they are. She has also had other spiritual experiences, such as seeing "the light" while in meditation and speaking to guides who have appeared to her as three-dimensional people and have given her messages.

It feels to me that this was a spiritual-opening dream that was obviously guided.

Recurring Dreams, Including Serial Dreams
Dream #21

> *My mom passed away last year. I keep having this dream off and on that she is knocking on the casket, asking to be let out.*

This is a fairly short dream. However, the dreamer shared that she had not been able to put this dream out of her mind and she was trying to figure out what it meant. She was concerned because friends of hers had told her that this dream was telling her that she hasn't let her mother go. Could this be why the dreamer has this dream on a recurring basis?

I'm not at all convinced that this is the case. I feel that this dream could have one of two possible meanings. The first is that the dreamer misses her mother so much that she wishes her mother hadn't died and might still be alive (in which case, in her dream, her mother could knock and ask to be let out). This is a natural reaction to the loss of a loved one and is part of the grieving process. Another possible (and certainly more grisly) interpretation would be that her mother wasn't truly dead when she was buried—that she, in essence, had been buried alive—and may have truly been knocking on the casket to get someone to let her out. I personally find that second interpretation and scenario to be highly unlikely and feel that the first of these two possible meanings is the true one.

The dreamer was very concerned about what her friends were telling her about this dream. As you may know, there is a fairly popular metaphysical concept that we can hold back passed-on loved ones from moving forward on the other side through grieving and missing them "too much." This would mean that the more intensely we miss a loved one (or the longer we grieve for them), the more our loved one, while on the other side, will be reluctant to move on to other levels. I personally don't buy into this concept. For one thing, I find it to be fear-based. This concept is "shoulding" people into feeling bad or guilty about their feelings of grief, whereas in reality, feeling grief is not only natural but also a natural part of the healing process after losing a loved one.

I feel it's important not to stay stuck in our grief and instead to allow ourselves to feel it while moving through it. Our loved ones have many things that they do, experience, and learn while on the other side (according to the information I've received over and over again whenever I've looked at the loved ones of clients who have transitioned). Those who have passed on know that their loved ones need to grieve and also have the ability to look in on and see what their loved ones still in body are doing. (In some ways, they can actually split their focus, project their energy, and even bilocate on the other side.)

So there's no need to feel any guilt about grieving. We are not holding our loved ones back through it. Even though there are some general stages of grief that many people go through, we may grieve in our own way. It's important to honor our feelings of loss, while knowing that the love between a loved one and us truly never dies.

This is a very poignant dream, because the dreamer truly misses her mother and appears to have been wracked by guilt through what others have told her. My wish for the dreamer is that she can understand that her grief is natural and for her to be kind to herself and less susceptible to others shoulding her. In time, as she moves further through the grieving process, she may have this dream less often.

Dream #22

I had a series of dreams involving my grandmother who had passed away many years earlier. In the first dream, she was chopping the left leg off roosters. They survived but hopped away bloodied. I was horrified and went to look for my mother asking her to stop my grandmother's cruelty. My mother just laughed at me, dismissing my concerns. In the last of the series of dreams, my grandmother and mother were visiting me in my apartment. To my surprise, my grandmother lay down on the floor, my mother behind her and holding her close as she sobbed. My grandmother was upset and frightened because she had cancer, which had started in her foot and spread up to her knee.

This series of dreams may be difficult to grasp at first glance. However, its meanings can be parsed out. The salient parts would seem to be the grandmother, mother, roosters, left leg, chopping, mother laughing and dismissive, grandmother sobbing, and cancer.

After the dreamer started having these dreams, she noticed a black spot on the back of her left leg. With this additional detail, the dreams' meanings may start to form.

The dreamer was no stranger to the idea that dreams can benefit us in our lives and can also give us information on health conditions. In fact, she had read Arnold Mindell's *Working with the Dreaming Body,* which focuses on the wisdom of both dreams and one's body for personal unfolding and growth and which includes the concept that physical symptoms can show up in dreams before they're actually in the body. The dreamer sensed that these dreams could be connected to the spot on her leg and were telling her that the spot could be malignant. She went to a doctor, who initially thought the spot was nothing to be concerned about. However, given her awareness of the power of dreams, the dreamer insisted on a biopsy, and a diagnosis of melanoma was then confirmed.

The doctor wanted to surgically remove a large portion of the dreamer's leg, but she resisted and subsequently found another doctor who was able to remove just the area around the spot. Her cancer was then gone and did not recur.

The story of her dream doesn't end there. She was able to use her intuition, information from another recurring dream she had had since childhood, and her research into healing to heal not just the melanoma on her leg, but also some emotional issues she had dealt with for years.

This particular recurring dream, then, was about her health and may also have represented visitations. What the dreamer did with these dreams is as an excellent example of how we can use information from our dreams to heal physical ailments and emotional and psychological issues. This is the true gift of dreams: to be able to use them as a tool in our lives for inner and outer healing and life improvement.

Spiritual Dreams, Including Awakening or Opening Dreams

Dream #23

I was a visitor with many others, especially women. We were all visiting a sacred ground, more specifically an ancient sculpture/statue, white stone, of a woman lying on her side. There was something else in the statue too, but I couldn't make it out. It was large and guarded by men in light beige/green uniforms and hats on their heads. They were wearing white gloves, as they were the only ones allowed to get near to touch anything. The statue had a natural low stone barrier around it creating a half-moon. The background was a tall wall, possibly stone/rock. Many people were there. As I approached this statue, something came over me.

Something happened to me. I was completely overcome by something, and it made me grasp for air and take a huge/very deep breath. I felt filled up with something/air/spirit, and as this happened, this woman statue opened her eyes in shock and disbelief.

She came alive like I had awakened her somehow. I started levitating, very confused but I felt like fairly calm. I "floated"/levitated away from her and then back toward her, and she was standing now. A priest approached me (he was also above ground). He looked at me with a serious look. I put my hands together to show him respect and then he smiled at me. He was dressed in a robe with all kinds of colors, predominantly gold/red and purple. High priest. Gray hair and beard. I floated above ground back to her and

asked, "Who I am? Whose soul/spirit do I have in me?"
She didn't answer. She just said, "I can't believe we
finally found you." I said, "How can I know what I am
supposed to do if I don't know who I am?"

She said, "You will know."

It was over, and I was back to "normal."

This is quite an interesting dream, isn't it? To me, it's
obviously a spiritual dream, with a spiritual setting and spiritual personages in it. It's possible that it was a real experience,
perhaps even taking place in another dimension, or was a
glimpse into a past life. Or perhaps it was a dream that wasn't
an actual experience and was, instead, just full of symbolism.

The dreamer is Annelie Pelfrey, whose husband had had
dream #6. She felt that the dream took place in the present,
rather than being a past-life experience, and that it felt like an
actual experience.

Clearly—at least to me—the woman/statue and men in
the dream were all spiritual figures and probably guides or
teachers to the dreamer. The dream is conveying a spiritual
message to her—either that she has spiritual abilities and/
or that she is in the process of awakening spiritually. The
dreamer levitating in the dream and the message given to
her that she is important and that they had been "waiting"
for her are indications to the dreamer of her spiritual significance or strength. Given the spiritual-awakening theme
of the dream, the statue coming to life may have represented
the dreamer, who is going from being asleep spiritually to
coming to life in a spiritual sense or reawakening even more
than she had previously. (In fact, we talk about people who

are "asleep" spiritually, and we refer to people who open up spiritually as "waking up.")

The dreamer asks who she really is (from a spiritual point of view) and then is told that she "will know." This is yet another indication that the dreamer is going through a process of spiritual awakening or shifting that is still unfolding, and her dream is obviously encouraging her in that process.

It's noteworthy that the dreamer has had similar spiritual dreams only in the past year. She has been working on her own spiritual growth and awareness as a result. There isn't much for the dreamer to do as a result of having had this powerful dream aside from continuing to pay attention to her dreams and continuing to unfold.

Dream #24

I was aware that I was asleep as my dream started. A small blue light appeared and grew larger, very similar to the way a camera lens works. As the blue light became larger, I found myself in a vast expanse of blue space. I was aware of a solid base under my feet, but I was unable to define an actual floor. Music surrounded me. It was more beautiful than anything I had ever heard. At first it was without words or source. It filled the vast space where I stood, and it wrapped around me in an almost physical blanket of sound.

A short time later, I noticed singing voices in the music and I turned to see who was singing. The first group I saw was babies in diapers and pajamas dancing and swinging. I could hardly believe what I was seeing. I kept asking myself, "How can tiny babies dance and sing like that?" A voice spoke: "The spirit sings."

I was led, but I couldn't see who was leading me, to another area of singing spirits. These people appeared to be very old, and some were sick, but their spirits were dancing with great energy and beauty as if they were young and healing.

I moved from one group to another, and I saw every type of person you can imagine, from the very old to the newborn babies all singing and dancing in the most joyous way. The atmosphere of love and peace permeated everything. A leader was with every group, and though I couldn't hear words being spoken or directions being given, I knew that the groups were being given instructions and encouragement.

When the blue light started to grow small, I was very sad. I wanted to stay in the place and join in with the music and dancing, but I was pulled back to my waking state.

This is another profound experience, a spiritual one, which took place during the dream state and represents a strong spiritual dream. The dreamer felt that this was an actual experience rather than her dreaming about being in a place like this. She said that she woke up from the dream feeling "complete joy and confidence" and that this feeling lasted for several days afterward. You might wonder what this "dream" was about.

The dreamer had some difficulty trying to frame what she had experienced in the dream, but was later told by one spiritual teacher that she had visited "etheric schools" and that everyone goes to them or is taken to them during the sleep state. The purpose of these schools, according to the teacher, is to give people encouragement and instruction on how to cope with our lives.

As we touched upon earlier, many people feel that we are worked with by guides and taken places while we're in the deepest levels of sleep and that we typically have no conscious memory of these experiences when we awaken. It would make sense that we would have no conscious memory of this. First of all, our state of consciousness is so deep that we would likely not have any conscious memory of this. Secondly, it's said that we may be taken to places that our human minds simply cannot conceive of, so we can't figuratively wrap our arms around the experiences.

When looking at clients' passed-on loved ones, I've often gotten that they will at times go to places of study where they are taught and learn new things. However, I've never gotten that the "classes" are made up only of people of the same age. So I feel that this dreamer's experience was not necessarily one of visiting these places of learning on the other side for those who have passed on as much as for those of us still in body.

This was a wonderful glimpse that the dreamer was given and represented yet another spiritual experience and gift. The dreamer shared that she's never gone back to that place again, but she now knows that it's there. What a lovely spiritual experience!

Combinations of Types

Dream #25

> *I dreamt the family (my four children and I) were on a Boy Scouts outing. We were downtown in a building when it got dark and lightning struck while we were looking out a window. There were four or five tornadoes off in the distance. We hurried and left, my boys in a different car from me. The wind was awful, and on the car radio there was a local weatherman talking about the trees and the wind. We decided for all in the Scouting group to drive to a nearby state and stay in a hotel. On the way, we were delayed by a stop at a vet clinic, although I don't know why. I saw people I knew with a sick cat, then I got a call from the hotel saying my debit card was declined (go figure!) and I couldn't reserve a room. Meanwhile, we had bad wind and weather conditions, and I was trying to reach my sister who could help with the hotel charge. I remember feeling different from everyone else, because they had no problems with booking their rooms. We still had bad windy conditions, my kids were still in another car with other Scouts, and in my head I remember thinking so logically [about] what else I could do to keep them safe. In my dream, I could see a vision of the hotel and us in it, but it was me thinking ahead, if that makes sense. Certain parts were very clear, colorful.*

This is quite a dream, almost verging on being a nightmare. Would you agree?

As you might guess, one of the first questions I posed to the dreamer was that of how she felt in the dream. Interestingly, she shared that she hadn't felt panicked, but perhaps mildly upset, and what was especially of interest was that she said that she kept having visions that everything would be okay.

Several things stand out in this dream. The bad weather is quite salient, of course, as are the obstacles in getting to a hotel, the dreamer's debit card being declined, her feeling different from the others in the dream, the help from her sister, and the dreamer being in a different car from her children. I asked the dreamer about some of this, and she said that she was going through some hurdles in her life.

This really resonated as probably being the overall meaning or backdrop of the dream, because the dreamer has some figurative "storms" in her life at present. Because of these challenges, the dreamer is likely feeling different from other people (because she may be assuming that others' lives are okay), and she may be looking to her sister for some assistance and also possibly feeling some distance from her children (or that her path in the present is different from that of her children), with them being in a separate car in her dream.

However, what is also significant is that she knows everything will be okay, because in her dream she keeps having a vision of arriving at her destination. And this might be the major thrust of the message in this dream for her—that despite the challenges she is facing in her life, she will indeed be okay.

From this point of view, it makes perfect sense that the storms, tornadoes, wind, etc., in her dream are merely the figurative "storms" she's facing in her life. However, to add a wonderful layer of complexity to her dream, she shared that several nights after she had this dream, there were strong, awful storms where she lives, similar to those in her dream. So her dream was precognitive and literal from the standpoint of letting her know that bad weather would be hitting the city in which she lived, while it was also symbolic and figurative in reflecting the figurative stormy weather in her life through the hurdles she was dealing with. Her unconscious may have intuitively picked up on the impending bad weather and then free-associated them with the figurative storms in the dreamer's life.

This is a wonderful example of the complexity some dreams have. This dream had a literal precognitive element, with the same detail also being symbolic, and it also expressed the dreamer's personal issues.

This dream served to let the dreamer know that she would be okay, while also reflecting to her that she does indeed feel different or separate from others. She can certainly consciously acknowledge and remind herself that she will be okay as she deals with the obstacles in her life, and she could also choose to work on her feeling different from others, if she chooses to.

This is a very helpful dream that I feel stems from the dreamer's unconscious and is reassuring for her at a time when she's going through some challenges.

Dream #26

I was dreaming that I was climbing a mountain, and I was one of a long line of people all hooked together by a rope. Every now and then someone would slip out of the rope and fall down the mountain and holler "AAAAHHHHHHHHH!!!," but the rest of us kept climbing. So every ten minutes or so, another person would slip through and I'd hear "AAAAHHHHHHHHH!!!" fading away. I woke up and I still heard "AAAAHHHHHHHH—" and it turned out to be my dad, who had taken the wrong turn and had slipped and fallen on the hardwood floor, and was calling out for someone.

At first glance, this dream appears to be an excellent example of how external conditions, such as noises, can be incorporated into and create or affect dream content and scenarios. When the dreamer woke up, there was indeed someone saying "aaaahhhh"—her father, who had slipped and fallen. This dream illustrates that phenomenon perfectly. However, aside from the fact that her father's calling out had influenced this dream, I felt that there were additional meanings, including two other possible salient ones.

The first would be that the dreamer could be involved in some sort of group effort that feels like an uphill climb, but that may be important enough that it's crucial that the other people keep going on and climbing. The other possible meaning would be that the dreamer feels there's some goal she has that feels like an uphill climb and is very difficult to attain.

When I asked the dreamer about these possibilities, she shared that there were indeed two situations in her life that fit those meanings and that resonated. The first was that she was looking for a summer job, something that she said she has to do every summer but that she feels is scary to contemplate due to the possibility of not finding one, and that it feels like a difficult prospect each summer.

The second situation had to do with her father, who was elderly. She was his main caretaker and shared that taking care of him felt like "an uphill slog" and that he was "sliding downhill very quickly," which was painful for her to observe and acknowledge.

This second meaning adds a strong element of poignancy to her dream and also amplifies the meaning of some of its details. When viewed from this second meaning having to do with her father, her dream also appears to be expressing the human condition, in which we, as humans, are always trying to climb and attain something higher (and perhaps attempting to move toward a spiritual goal). However, it is the nature of life that some people die (slip and fall off the mountain), sometimes prematurely. From this perspective, her dream is also expressing the interconnectedness of life, because all the people who are climbing this mountain—as a metaphor for moving through life—are "hooked together by a rope," implying that we're all in this together.

I feel that there was more than one source of this dream and that it came from an external source (her father's cries), as well as from her unconscious and possibly also her higher soul awareness, given the profound spiritual metaphor.

This was a marvelous, powerful dream that was illustrating more than one thing—how external noises can affect and be woven into dream content, two difficult situations that the dreamer found herself in in real life, and her pathos over her father's deteriorating condition—and a beautiful, poignant, and philosophical metaphor for life itself.

A powerful dream!

———

These dream samples should give you a better sense of the different types of dreams, and the interpretations provided for each should allow you to gain a sense of each dream's meanings and how to interpret dreams.

Next I'll share some dreams for you to practice interpreting.

seven

Your Turn: Dreams for You to Interpret

I'll share some dreams with you in this chapter that you can practice interpreting. I realize that you won't be able to dialogue with the dreamer yourself, but I'll include information I gleaned from doing so, where appropriate. You also won't be able to hear the dream recounted and the tone of voice and any inflections that stand out. Don't let that deter you, however, as you should still be able to glean some meanings.

As you read these dreams, make sure you use the tips and the step-by-step procedure I shared in chapter 5, as well as your intuition. Once you've interpreted the dreams, you can turn to the end of this chapter, where you'll find the interpretations that I made for each one. I'll include these dreams in no particular order.

Dreams

Dream #27

This morning I had an interesting dream. I dreamed that a werewolf was in the house after me and that my husband was just sitting there. I was running all through the house trying to get away and then I woke up. Once I woke up I realized the werewolf was a German shepherd, my totem animal, and I'm puzzled why I was afraid of her and thought she was a werewolf.

When I asked the dreamer how she had felt, she shared that she did indeed feel fear, that her job had gotten extremely stressful, and that she was feeling overwhelmed.

Dream #28

I saw last night in my dream that I was throwing up in my room :(and I was even able to smell it. Then my mom came and suggested that I open the balcony's door so the smell would go away. I threw up all at once!!

Dream #29

I have had numerous dreams over the past 10+ years about learning/ furthering my education. The overall "theme" of my dreams is that I am very eager to learn new things, but the people around me keep trying to convince me that I should enroll in a course/program which I have no interest in doing. They don't believe

I am capable of doing what I have decided is best for me. This describes the attitude of most of my family members.

The dreamer shared that she doesn't live in proximity to her family members and doesn't communicate with them very often.

Dream #30

I had another weird dream about my ex. In the dream, a clairvoyant put our pictures together and drew a heart around it and then said to me, "Go and find him." (Errr, I know where he is and he's married—crikey!) The dream was full-on, though.

The dreamer shared that she's had other dreams in which her ex tells her that he loves her and not his present wife. She further shared that she and her ex split due to outside pressure and not because they weren't doing well together—and, further, that he had seemed to marry on the rebound.

Dream #31

In this dream, I was in a low-rise urban area and an earthquake was striking. The buildings were falling to rubble and the earth was cracking open, but I had no fear. A "guardian" was walking me through the various ways I may die in this scenario and helping me figure out the ways to make the most of my last moments, such as, if the earth opened and I were falling, would I be stoic and silent or enjoy the last feel of my body by yelling as loud as I could? I chose to yell. People were being sifted into the ground and were head deep. The walls of buildings were diagonal "shards," and all were broken to the ground in some way. When the "training" was over, I woke up calm and stoic.

Dream #32

My daughter had a scary dream at the beginning of the year. She woke up and said, "Mom, what's melanoma?" She didn't know what that was, but had dreamt that her dad had "melanoma" on his scalp where his hair was.

Despite the part in the dream about the dreamer's father (who is a medical doctor) having melanoma, it turned out that he didn't.

Dream #33

I was in a foreign country with some friends. We ran into some terrorists there who were trying to intimidate me. I decided to stand my ground and not cave in to their demands. Somebody in my group suggested that I go into the woods. I said that I had tried that before and didn't want to do that again. But I ended up there again. While I was in the woods, I saw a house across a field. I decided to go to the house and crossed the field quickly so I wouldn't be seen by the terrorists. I couldn't find a way in at the back and then had to go around the house to get to the front. It was newer and large and spacious and I was able to go into it.

The dreamer shared that she was going through a very difficult time financially after her husband passed away.

Dream #34

I had one of those "real" dreams that let you know there is a deep meaning for you. I was selling a house and I moved out (an older home), but I was younger than I am now and had a child, a boy. (I have a grown daughter in this lifetime.) I went back into the house to check on some things. I had allowed another friend to let her small dog stay in the house until she also moved. However, upon returning, I saw that the dog had done his business on the floor and my friend had not been there to clean up the mess, so I did. She showed up, and I had to ask her to please take the dog out of the house, even though it was difficult for me to ask her to do this because I really wanted to help her out.

Then a man came in who I found that I was interested in and somehow we knew each other. He came to the house and, without letting me know ahead of time, had invited several of his friends to come over for a party, even though the house was empty. He was totally unaware that I was interested in him. (I found this interesting and I haven't been interested in having a relationship for a long time…I'm very happy being single.) But in the dream I was very much wanting his attention, but he was not showing any interest in me. He was young and handsome and I was trying to coordinate all the things you have to do when selling a house, and I had forgotten to have the electricity, etc. turned off in the midst of dealing with the friend's dog

and having this gentleman invite people over for a party
at the house.

My cell phone was also involved, because for some
reason it would not "charge," and this was unlike me not
to have it charged. I woke up feeling really confused, but
all these details really made me take note of the dream.

There's a lot going on in this dream. Rather than try to figure out all the details in it right away, try to read it over
again to gain a feel for it, and look for any common threads
running through it.

Dream #35

I dreamed that I visited a place whose doors opened
inwards, and, when they closed, the doors became one
with the walls. There was no exit. My mother sat at
a table sorting stones to be used in a spiral patterned
walkway. She looked up and said, "What are you doing
here? You're not due here for a long time yet."

I was surrounded by young men in white shirts and
black pants, all eager to help me do anything but get
out. I started to panic that I could not exit this weird
walled, door-free structure, and every time I saw my
mother, she would reject my presence.

It would be helpful for you to know that the dreamer's
mother had already passed several years before the dreamer
had this dream.

Dream #36

This morning, I dreamed that there was a bear in our house. (My children and I live with their grandmother.) We were all in our bedroom. She locked the door and thought we'd be safe. I would not even indulge in the idea. Immediately, I opened the windows, kicked out the screen, and started ushering us out of the window. I asked the minis if they knew where to meet. They said, "Yes, the playground." As I was running toward the playground, I realized there was no one running behind me and I kept running. It was nighttime. Stars were visible. There were people outside at the playground when I arrived. They were hanging out listening to music that was playing in their cars. I asked a man if I could use his phone to call 911. I got the sense that the children were on the playground waiting for me, but I never saw them in the dream. Even when we were in the house before I opened the window, I didn't see them. I only knew they were there.

It turned out that the dreamer thought of two different types of bears whenever she thought of a bear, both Winnie the Pooh and a raging bear (as in the phrase "he's a real bear"). She also sometimes refers to her children as the "minis."

Dream #37

I find myself in a huge auditorium setting, surrounded by hundreds of people… all waiting for the Leader to appear and speak. I determine that this is some type of charismatic cult situation, but did not realize this until this point in the dream. I had been invited to hear a "lecture" and was told this would change my life forever. Out of curiosity, I had decided to attend. All ages are here ... male and female, also. People are dressed in various types of uniforms of different colors. I learn that the clothing designates your rank in the organization. It's clear that this is some sort of mind-control situation. I find it ludicrous that clothing is being used to rank members in a hierarchy and how absurd it is that anyone would believe some people are better or more important than others.

Just before the Leader arrives, I think it best to get out quickly but don't want to draw attention to myself, so I quietly slip out of the seat and walk back to the entrance through a maze-like series of long hallways. Once there, I see that I must exit through a full-body turnstile and turn over my purse to a security guard in the "cage." I'm not allowed to leave unescorted. One of the members, a male, assures me I will be given back my purse, but first he will take me across the street for coffee.

While there, I intuitively realize the guard is stealing my personal information, fingerprints, etc., from the purse in order to be able to track me after I'm released. I now understand that they will never let you just walk away once you've seen inside the operation/cult.

The dreamer shared that she has been in a relationship that appears to be getting more serious.

Dream #38—First Dream

I've had three dreams recently that all involved a large body of water. In the first one, I was in a river and I was swimming toward a shore where everyone I know was gathered. The current was strong, and I couldn't get to the water's edge. I called for help, but no one heard. As I went under, two people walked out to me on top of the water. One was my husband. As he got closer, he became more submerged, until the water was up to his waist when he reached me. I was looking up at them from underneath the water and furious that they were not reaching out to help me. They just looked at me underneath the water. I struggled to reach the surface but couldn't do it. I didn't understand how they could be on top of the water.

I woke up in a panic. But later I couldn't help but wonder what would've happened if I had just let go and allowed myself to go with the current.

Dream #38—Second Dream

I was playing in the ocean with my family, and there were hundreds of other people swimming and playing in the water as well. I looked down in the water and saw an old artifact of some kind. I was focused on trying to move it with my foot and was not paying attention to what was going on around me. Suddenly

*the water stopped moving and became very still. I
looked up and saw large black ships moving toward the
shore. My family was gone. Hundreds of people were
gone. There were only a few of us left. No bodies—just
gone. We ran out of the water. I was searching for my
family everywhere. I met a neighbor from twenty years
ago. She just looked at me point blank and said, "Don't
you know you are supposed to lead those of us who are
left?" I began to sob as hard as I've ever cried in real
life. Then I woke up.*

Dream #38—Third Dream

*From last night. This was on a lake. There was a big,
elaborate puppet show in a floating stage a ways off
shore. The community floated out on various boats,
rafts, floats, etc., with their kids and picnics to watch
the show. I was enchanted by the presentation. All
I had to get out to the presentation was a surfboard-
like skiff. I made it out there just fine and found some
friends who were on a nice houseboat, but they didn't
invite me to join them. The water became choppy
from all of the boats and I was getting tossed around. I
couldn't see the show, my nice clothes got soaked, and
I slid off the board. I couldn't get back on and had to
hold the board and kick my way back to shore. I could
hear people laughing and enjoying the show as I made
my way back. There's more, but I don't remember it.*

These three dreams are related and there are commonalities among them, one of which is water. I asked the dreamer

what water signified for her, and she shared that water has always represented spirituality to her. So in these three dreams the dreamer is immersed in spirituality.

Dream #39

> *I had a dream last night that I went into the chicken coop to gather eggs. To my surprise, the rooster was nesting and had laid two eggs, both fertilized. The rooster had accidentally cracked one open from laying [sic] on it. I knew it wouldn't mature, but the other was fine.*
>
> *The night before I had a dream that a lot of men were getting pregnant. I couldn't figure out how they would give birth, but stopped worrying because, if they could conceive, then there was a natural way to give birth. Even if I didn't understand.*
>
> *I was wondering if these two dreams were related. The same night I dreamt of men getting pregnant my daughter had the same dream. We do that a lot.*

I asked the dreamer if she had any projects going on, and she shared that she did—two different work projects, in fact.

Dream #40

> *I was living in a HUGE turn-of-the-20th-century house (not a mansion, but close enough) with a female roommate. There were six men trying to break in on us, but I could only see two. They taunted me/us as they made their way in, and I talked smack to them*

right back. They weren't there to rob us or rape us; they were just breaking in to play a twisted cat-and-mouse game, and I felt strongly that they planned to kill us when they were done.

The first one, the ringleader, made his way in. His demeanor was very relaxed and teasing, sort of like the Joker (only not as boisterous as Jack Nicholson's and not as dark and deadpan as Heath Ledger's.... He was somewhere in between).

He and I bantered back and forth (he was trying to throw me off balance; I was just talking smack and cussing him out) while I beat him with martial arts and any and everything I could get my hands on. His voice and demeanor never wavered as we fought and he threatened to attack my roommate. I finally got the drop on him and bludgeoned him to death.

I ran through the house looking for my roommate and easily killed the second guy along the way. Apparently, before I ran into him, he had set the house on fire. I put the fire out, called 911, found my roommate (who had already called them herself), then together we found the other four guys in a room, dead from either smoke inhalation or because I had blacked out and killed them (my memory is unclear). The police and fire departments arrived shortly afterwards, and then I woke up.

The violence and feeling of personal threat are so evident in this dream that one might conclude that the dreamer felt fear during it. When queried, though, the dreamer hadn't felt afraid during the dream or upon awakening. She shared that she had just completed a personal development course.

Dream #41

Just before my dream started, I thought, "I'm asleep." Just as that thought formed, a light appeared in front of me and opened much like the lens of a camera. I saw my father sitting at a table a few feet in front of me. He was smiling. I felt so comforted to see him, and I wanted to run to him and give him a hug.

"Hello, Daughter!" he greeted me. "I am going to wait right here until your book is published!"

I noticed that hardback books were stacked on the table on either side of him. There was something odd about them, because all I could see was their outline, as if they weren't completed or formed yet. My father looked down and began writing on one of the transparent books as though he were signing autographs at a typical book-signing event.

I looked around, and there were no other people there and the room itself was not fully furnished. As I looked more closely, the only thing that looked solid in this space was my father. The camera lens suddenly closed and the dream ended.

Dream #42

I had a dream last week that featured a bedroom that filled with water like a bathtub. After I drained it, a woman I assumed was my mother came in the room dressed head to toe in crabgrass green, '70s style. And the role of my mother was played by Meryl Streep.

The dreamer shared that she'd had ongoing difficult issues with her mother.

―――――

Now here are the interpretations to the previous dreams. Compare your interpretations with mine, and see how much information you were able to get, as well as any clues in the dreams that you—or I—may have overlooked.

Interpretations

Dream #27 Interpreted

This sounds like it was a scary dream and illustrates the need to ask about the emotions the dreamer felt in the dream. I asked the dreamer how she had felt during the dream, and she did indeed feel fear. This confirmed that it was a problematic scenario for her, but more interpretation was required.

In looking at this dream, you may be struck by the werewolf in the dream and feel that it could be the most significant aspect of the dream. I was more struck, however, by the juxtaposition between the dreamer's fear and her husband's nonchalant attitude. I then asked her if she ever felt that her husband didn't relate to, understand, or sympathize with her fears or problems. As it turned out, at the time she had this dream, the dreamer was feeling that her job had gotten extremely stressful, that she was completely overwhelmed by it all, *and* that her husband just didn't seem to understand what she was going through. So from this perspective, this dream was indeed expressing how the dreamer felt that her husband might have been oblivious to her plight.

Of course, the fact that it was a werewolf chasing her in the dream did have some significance. She felt upon awakening that it had been her dog, a German shepherd, who had morphed into the werewolf. The significance is that something seemingly everyday and nonthreatening—her job—had morphed into a figurative "monster" that was pursuing and overwhelming her.

There seemed to be two issues that her dream was revealing to her: her job having gotten overwhelming and her husband's seeming lack of empathy. So there were two areas of discomfort that her unconscious was revealing to her that needed to be dealt with in some way in order for her to have a feeling of wholeness restored. Thus, this was a dream that may have needed to be followed up on in some way, perhaps by discussing with her boss how she was feeling about her job, discussing with her husband her feeling that he was unsympathetic, etc. Because the scenario in the dream was somewhat extreme and elicited her fear and feeling pursued, it would seem that it was asking her to take action in some way.

Dream #28 Interpreted

This is a fairly short dream, which on the face of it could be literal or symbolic.

This is another good example of how much more information we can derive from dialogue with the dreamer. To me, it felt that the situation in the dream was figurative and that there was potentially a situation in the dreamer's life that was sickening her, whether literally or figuratively. When I asked her if she was dealing with anything like that, she confirmed that she was and that there was a situation that she had gotten "sick of" and that she felt needed clearing up.

In her dream, she was doing just that. She was expelling the situation from her body (and from affecting her space). In fact, she cleared up the situation all at once—by vomiting it out all at once rather than in a prolonged and drawn-out fashion. Her last sentence in her dream account, "I threw up all at once!," feels to me as if she was surprised by this.

There is a detail in the dream that I also feel is significant, and that is that the dreamer could smell the vomit in the dream—quite obviously an unpleasant smell. Do you know what that could mean? I feel that it's indicating that the situation the dreamer is facing in real life is a "smelly" one, figuratively speaking. This alludes to our referring to situations as "fishy" or smelling bad. You'll note that this dream (stemming, I'm sure, from the dreamer's unconscious) takes the figurative feel of the situation and translates it in the dream into something literal. (Remember, your unconscious loves puns and plays on words.)

This detail is significant, because, if the dreamer in real life had doubts about whether the situation was okay or not, her dream is letting her know that it's a smelly one that has sickened her. In fact, she shared that she felt relieved after throwing up in the dream.

So this dream is giving the dreamer insight and clarity on a real-life situation that she is unsure what to do about or how to handle. The dreamer may then take this information and insight and take action on the problematic situation. It's a very useful dream!

Make sure not to discount a dream that's really short by thinking that it couldn't have much meaning or significance for you due to its brevity. Some dreams can pack a lot of meaning into a short scenario.

Dream #29 Interpreted

These are obviously difficult dreams for the dreamer to have, especially given that she really wants to learn new things. The dreamer feels that she is quite well aware of how unsupportive her family is and is perplexed as to why she continues to have these dreams. Did you get any insight on this?

Given that her family doesn't live in proximity to the dreamer, what could be triggering these dreams?

Remember that our unconscious, I feel, is our greatest inner ally and tries to bring us to balance and wholeness. If there is something that is bothering us—an unresolved issue, for example—our unconscious may yield this up to us in dreams. It's as if our unconscious is telling us, when we have dreams about those unresolved issues, "Hey, here's something that's still bothering you."

Having family members not be supportive of us is extremely difficult. Our family is who we would tend to turn to *for* support in our lives. They are supposed to be the people we are closest to. So when family members are not supportive and when it seems that, to the contrary, they have rejected us or turned against us, it's quite painful.

It feels that this is what these repeated dreams are about. As it turned out, the dreamer had just endured another apparent insult from a family member who had ignored her, and this could have been the trigger for the dream.

In a situation like this, when it seems that our unconscious is tapping us on the shoulder and asking us to work on resolving a difficult situation like this, what can we do? Changing the attitude of family members would be a difficult task, one that may seem insurmountable (and usually is). We could try talk therapy or counseling, as well as various healing modalities, such as EFT. (You'll find a longer list of healing modalities in appendix A.) Until we're able to resolve the issue for ourselves and get to a place where the issue has been defused or no longer bothers us on any level, dreams such as this may continue to happen. It's a difficult situation for the dreamer to be in.

Dream #30 Interpreted

To me, given the fact that the dreamer has had many dreams about her ex in which he tells her that he still loves her, I would wonder if the dream isn't a message to her that he will be back in her life again one day. If the dreamer had had this one dream just once, then I would say it would be less likely that the dream was conveying this information. However, the dreamer has had persistent dreams conveying this same message.

The dreamer has been trying to go on with her life, and it sounds like these dreams are intruding on her decision to do just that. However, the persistence of these dreams would appear to indicate that things may change at some point in the future, although it will take time to see what does indeed transpire.

So where could this dream be stemming from, especially given that the dreamer consciously feels a discomfort with the dream's message? It could still be stemming from her unconscious, but it feels more likely to me that it stems from a guide, or the dreamer's higher soul awareness, or even a passed-on loved one.

The question then arises as to what to do with information like this from a dream about a relationship that has ended. Do you listen to the dream and sit around and wait? Or do you try to file the information from the dream away and still go on with your life? This is always a matter of personal preference, but I would opt for the second choice. It's problematic, first of all, to tie up your energy in an eventuality that may never materialize—*and,* if a relationship will indeed be rekindled at some point in the future, sitting around and waiting for it to happen is less than healthy. It may be best to go on with your life and see what develops, including with someone else.

I do intuitively feel that the dreamer's ex will reappear, and at the same time I applaud her decision to go on with her life. It will be interesting to see what might manifest over time.

Dream #31 Interpreted

This dream seems to have an apocalyptic feel to it and seems to be about an aspect of Earth changes—strong earthquakes. There's a spiritual element to this dream with the "guardian" (representing a guide or guardian angel) walking with the dreamer through the scene and guiding him and asking him questions.

It's hard to say whether this is a precognitive dream or one representing fears on the part of the dreamer about any possibly impending Earth changes.

The positive thing is that the dreamer woke up feeling "calm and stoic," as opposed to fearful. That element could indicate that the dream was preparing the dreamer for Earth changes, either for going through them or for being less affected emotionally by them taking place because of the dream rehearsal. This dream could also represent spiritual training that the dreamer is receiving, as the guardian in the dream appears to be both guiding and training him. This would then attest to the spiritual orientation of the dreamer and the need for him to be trained and prepared spiritually in some way and for some reason. No follow-up action or work would appear to be needed.

Dream #32 Interpreted

This dream is quite interesting, because the girl dreamed of "melanoma" even though she didn't even consciously know what it was and hadn't heard of the word.

We would usually turn to an obvious meaning of this dream, namely that the girl had intuitively picked up on a health condition of her father's. However, as mentioned, it turned out that the girl's father did not have melanoma or any other skin condition.

The girl's mother shared that about ten months after her daughter had this dream, the girl decided that she wanted to be a doctor and to enroll in college as pre-med after she graduated from high school. And what the girl wanted to specialize in was cosmetic dermatology. (Since the girl's father is a medical doctor, that may have been the basis in her dream

for her father having melanoma, as he was a link unconsciously for her to the field of medicine.) We don't know if
the girl's dream and later decision to become a cosmetic der-
matologist are related, but I suspect they are.

Given that the girl had never heard of the word "melanoma," her dream about it feels as if it was given to her. In all
likelihood, a guide may have triggered this dream, although
it could also have come from her higher soul awareness. It's
also possible that her father communicated this dream to her
as a message, even if unconsciously.

This example illustrates that we have to look at each
dream individually in order to determine its meanings.
After all, this dream was not about a health issue that someone known to the dreamer had, but instead was about her
own career path, complete with a word in it that was utterly
unknown to her at the time. This is a marvelously intuitive
dream that was quite helpful and insightful!

Dream #33 Interpreted

What do you make of this dream? It has several different elements to it, including being in a foreign country, being with
friends, terrorists, intimidation, standing ground, being in
some woods, a house, not finding a way to enter at the back,
entering through the front, and the house being newer and
large and spacious. Did you pick up on any of these elements
being significant and, if so, what their meanings could be?

I personally feel that all of these elements are important ones to focus on and determine the meanings of, and
we can determine some overall meanings of this dream
through doing that, if we dialogue with the dreamer to get
full meanings.

Given that the dreamer was facing economic problems, were you able to determine what her dream could be indicating?

First of all I feel that it's significant that at the beginning of this dream the dreamer finds herself in a "foreign" country. To me, this is indicating that she's finding herself in a foreign place or situation, meaning that the financial bind she finds herself in is foreign to her. Having to navigate her way through the financial strictures and negotiations with creditors was also foreign territory to her. One good thing in the dream is that she's not alone. She's with friends who can be supportive of her.

Who could the terrorists be who are trying to intimidate her? I feel that the terrorists represent her husband's and her creditors who are acting like terrorists in using tactics to intimidate her. She herself may feel very scared by this situation and by the creditors' tactics because of the word "terrorists." I feel that it's alluding not just to the tactics the creditors are using, but also to the fear that the dreamer is feeling as a result of their actions and the situation that she now finds herself in.

In spite of the fear she's feeling and the tactics of intimidation that the creditors are using, the dreamer decides not to cave in to them and, instead, to stand her ground.

One of her friends suggests that the dreamer "go into the woods." What could this mean?

In the context of the dream, it would appear to mean either hiding out or hunkering down and waiting for the danger to pass. Being in the woods can also evoke a fear of getting lost in the woods. Either way, the dreamer says that she had tried that before and doesn't want to do that again. This detail would seem to indicate that being in the woods may refer to being passive and either hiding or waiting. In spite of her not wanting to do this again, she does end up doing it.

We don't know how long she's been hiding and/or waiting in the woods, but she sees a house across the field in front of the woods. For some reason, she's drawn to the house. So the house must represent some type of sanctuary or even a solution to her. It's a goal she wants to reach. In order to reach that goal, she has to leave her hiding place in the woods and risk being seen by or visible to the terrorists (her creditors), but she decides to take that risk.

While she's still out in the open and visible (i.e., isn't under the cover of the woods), she makes her way quickly to the house and, more specifically, to the back of the house. However, in this position, she's unable to get into the house. She then realizes that she needs to try the front of the house. What could all this mean?

I feel that she can't figuratively go in the back door of her solution. Having to go in the back can evoke a "back-door approach," not being of enough stature to enter through the front, or not being able to be direct. I intuitively felt that this had more to do with stature and being good enough to go in the front, as well as being direct.

So this house appears to be a solution, but what does it signify?

Given the fact that the house is "newer and large and spacious," it feels to me that it represents a new mindset. From this point of view, when the dreamer goes around to the front door, the dream is indicating that she needs to find a way to feel more worthy so that she can get to a new place and that, once she's there, it will be larger and more spacious for her and/or that she needs to develop a new and more spacious mindset. Interestingly, the dreamer shared that there's a business that she has wanted to start for some time, but has procrastinated about doing so.

With this in mind, it would appear that this dream is encouraging her to work on her mindset in order to feel more worthy and is giving her a message that she needs to start on this new venture.

There's a lot of information in this dream that is giving the dreamer insight. She's being encouraged to stand up to the creditors and not cave in or cower. She has support from friends, and she needs to work on feeling worthy. She needs to move toward that new mindset that will be more expansive for her, and to start her new business.

This dream is a highly symbolic one, with strong messages for the dreamer. It feels to me that it's partly coming from the dreamer's unconscious, with some parts coming from guides or other loving and supportive beings. It's a wonderfully encouraging dream for the dreamer that's telling her to persevere even though she's in a very difficult situation.

Dream #34 Interpreted

Did you sense the pervading theme of feeling put upon by other people? This feels like a strong theme running through this dream.

Note that the dream takes place in a house, an "older home," that the dreamer was selling and had moved out of. What could that mean?

If we substitute a way of being or one's mind for a house, we find that the house represents her former or "older" way of being. In real life, the dreamer has undergone a lot of personal growth and has learned to erect boundaries and not let others in her life take advantage of her or soil her inner terrain (or where she lives). The house in her dream, however, represents her former way of being.

If the dreamer has grown past this habit of letting others take advantage of her, one has to wonder why she has had this dream. When asked, the dreamer shared that she had had an incident the day prior to having this dream that involved someone whom the dreamer felt had been invading her boundaries and trying to use her. Can you see why she might have had this dream as a result and how that real-life situation served to elicit this dream?

It would appear that the unpleasant situation with the person had triggered for the dreamer the memory of what things had been like when she, figuratively speaking, had been living in that older home—i.e., what things had been like when she used to let people take advantage of her. On some level, she may have had an unconscious fear, given the incident the day before, that she might be reverting to that way of life, living without boundaries and letting others use her or take advantage of her kind nature.

It's interesting that in the first part of the dream the dreamer has already moved and is helping a friend who has not yet moved. So the dream at that point is referring to the dreamer (even though she has "moved"—i.e., moved past her pattern of not establishing boundaries with others) helping a friend who has not yet grown to the point where she establishes boundaries or is past the point of intruding upon or taking advantage of others. So the dreamer knows that it's helpful to erect boundaries, whereas her friend has not yet learned this. You'll note the detail of the dreamer feeling that it was difficult for her to ask her friend to take the dog out of the house, meaning that the dreamer still found it difficult at times to erect boundaries.

The second part of the dream also has some interesting details. Consider that the dreamer is being prevailed upon by a very handsome man. The dreamer states that she hasn't been interested in a relationship in a long time, but in her dream she is interested in this man. Did you notice anything noteworthy in this part of the dream?

I found her statement that she "was very much wanting his attention" to be significant. Often when we haven't grown to the point at which we accept and embrace ourselves, we look to others for attention and validation. In real life, the dreamer had grown past this, but in the dream she has regressed to this former way of being and was looking to this handsome man for attention/validation. It's significant that the dreamer forgot to turn the electricity off. Given that this appears right after the part about the man, it may be referring to the dreamer having forgotten to tamp down her sexual "electricity."

There's another detail in the dream that would appear to have significance. Do you know which one it is?

It's the detail about her cell phone that would not charge. In fact, it's the word "charge" that stands out, and the dreamer had even put the word in quotation marks in her write-up of her dream. We could say that her phone not being charged meant that it wouldn't work, but charge also evokes being in charge. The latter is what feels significant, because in the dream she didn't feel in charge of the situation and hadn't taken charge of her life, including her inner life.

So this dream would appear to have been triggered by the dreamer's real-life encounter with the friend who was taking advantage of her. It's possible that the dreamer may have felt some guilt about breaking her association with this person, guilt perhaps that she should help the person. If so, her dream is reminding her of what her inner life had felt like in the past when she used to allow people to invade her space and take advantage of her and that growing past that pattern has actually been good for her.

The dreamer knew that her personal growth and having erected personal boundaries with others had helped her, and her dream was reminding her of this. I feel that it most likely stemmed from the dreamer's unconscious and is an excellent example of how your unconscious can give you messages about your own personal unfolding and guide you, and serve a helpful role for you in your life.

Dream #35 Interpreted

This dream would appear to be a very symbolic one, with parts of it being an actual experience. Even though it's a fairly short dream, it would appear to be meaningful for the dreamer, as it seemed to elicit some strong emotions for her. Were you able to get a sense of what it might mean?

I feel that the dreamer was visiting the afterlife in this dream. Perhaps she had been chewing on what the afterlife might be like, and in reality the dreamer's father had passed away less than a year prior to her having this dream. Some clues in her dream that she was visiting the other side include her mother being there, of course, and the fact that once one entered the place, one could not exit, because the doors only opened inward. It's quite noteworthy that the dreamer wrote in the early part of her dream that "the doors became one with the walls." "To be one with" is a phrase that definitely evokes spirituality. Another telling detail is that of the "spiral patterned walkway" that the dreamer's mother is working on. A spiral has spiritual flavors and connotations, as there are spiritual concepts about moving upward in a spiral. So this dream, to me, most definitely has a spiritual context.

One of the most significant details in this dream, I feel, is her mother saying to her, "You're not due here for a long time yet." This is very similar to the message that some people who have had a near-death experience receive during their NDE when they're told that "it's not your time yet" or "you have more work to do."

The detail of the young men who are very eager to help the dreamer but who are unable to help her exit is an interesting one. I'm not convinced that it's hugely important, but it does convey that those who are in this place—the afterlife—are friendly and eager to help, even if they're not guides.

What is additionally significant is the dreamer's reaction in the dream. She panics because she's unable to leave this place. She also feels rejected by her mother. There could be more than one meaning of these dream segments. The first is that she misses her mother, but that the only way for the dreamer to visit her mother would be for her to go to the afterlife herself (i.e., die), and, if she does that, she would not be able to return to life (given that the doors open only inward, with no exit). Another meaning is that the dreamer may have an underlying feeling, one that could have existed for years, that she has been rejected by her mother, and/or that her mother doesn't want to have much to do with her, and/or that she is unworthy of being with her mother.

What starts out as a dream in which the dreamer is given a positive message that it's not her time yet and that she has a lot more time to live then morphs into a less-than-positive expression of feelings of rejection from her mother.

The dreamer could separate the two messages in this dream and affirm the first message in a positive way, while also working on the underlying negative feeling of rejection by her mother. It would really be up to the dreamer to know what resonates from this dream and how to approach working on anything being shown to her.

It's a fascinating dream that appears to be quite mixed, with a positive spiritual message alongside an expression of the dreamer's underlying fear. This dream could partly be a real experience in which the dreamer visited with her mother and partly an expression of underlying fear, the latter of which would be stemming from the dreamer's unconscious. The wonderful thing is that the dreamer could always work on any underlying feelings of rejection or unworthiness.

Dream #36 Interpreted

This is an interesting dream that turned out to have a surprising meaning! Do you have a sense of the meaning of this dream from reading it?

In spite of the scenario, it seemed as if the bear in the house was perhaps the most significant detail in the dream. Do you have a sense of what the bear could signify? Determining its meaning required dialoguing with the dreamer.

It's obvious from the dream that the dreamer is trying to get her children (whom she refers to at times as the "minis") away from the bear and to safety, because the bear represents a threat to their safety. (A playground may signify safety to her, as that's where children play.)

When pressed about who or what the bear (with two different sides to the bear personality, both Winnie the Pooh and a raging bear) could refer to, the dreamer realized that it was herself. She said she could be very sweet and loving, but then at times start to rage and be like a tornado. It's interesting that in the dream she knows her children are there, but cannot see them. This detail could be indicating that when she's angry and raging, she can't even see her children, because she gets so caught up in her anger (as in a "blind rage"). She wants to get them to safety, and their grandmother even tries to protect them, so there are good intentions. It's just that the bear is a menace when it (she) is raging.

The children's grandmother is also prominent in the dream. What role does she play in the meaning of the dream? It turned out that the dreamer wasn't comfortable living with her mother-in-law, and that was likely contributing to her anger.

So the dream was giving the dreamer a message about her effect on her children when she's angry, that they need to be protected from that side of her—a very sobering message!

The dream could also be giving the dreamer some insight into the fact that living with her mother-in-law contributes to her anger. This insight could lead the dreamer to reevaluate living there.

This dream could have come from the dreamer's unconscious, a guide, or her higher soul awareness, and it's a well-intentioned dream that is trying to give the dreamer insight that could be helpful for her, as well as for her children. This dream is one that may be pointing to action the dreamer can take; i.e., determining what is causing her anger, which could be physiological (as in low sugar levels) or psychological, and working on the cause of her anger issues.

Dream #37 Interpreted

The dreamer felt that this dream had an important message for her that she was struggling to decipher. I asked her if there was anything going on in her life at present that felt like a form of conforming or mind control, and she immediately answered that it was a relationship she was involved in.

Take a look at the dream again now that you know it has to do with a relationship issue and see what you get out of it.

Clearly she's concerned about the issue of conformity and being controlled, but there are other elements as well.

It's interesting that the dreamer shared that she hadn't even been consciously thinking about these issues in the relationship until after she shared the dream with me and we looked for which area of her life it related to. So this dream is giving her a heads-up about issues that were simmering in her unconscious that she wasn't consciously aware of.

In the dream, she's going to hear a lecture, which indicates something that she'll gain and learn from and one that should be life-altering in a positive way. When we spoke about her dream, the dreamer shared that the aspect of the lecture in the dream changing her life and the implicit promise of it solving all her problems really resonated with her. She realized that that implicit promise had been a trap for her in her previous relationships (the feeling that if she were in a relationship, her problems would be solved) and that she was determined not to fall into that seeming trap again.

In her dream, she decides to attend "out of curiosity." It's the type of event that has mass appeal, as there are all age groups there and both males and females. This may be speaking to the universal appeal of being in a relationship with someone and may or may not imply that there is a mass appeal about a relationship solving all of one's problems.

However, the dreamer is dismayed to realize that people are wearing uniforms and that there is a designated hierarchy according to color of the clothing. I asked the dreamer if clothing had been an issue in her relationship, and she acknowledged that she hadn't realized before that her partner may have been wanting for her to change her customary style of clothing. She preferred a more casual dressy style that is somewhat classy, but was sensing that her partner wanted her to wear a sexier style that she wasn't completely comfortable with.

At this point in the dream, the dreamer decides that she doesn't want to stay in this atmosphere and gets up to exit. However, exiting is not easy, as she has to go though "a maze-like series of long hallways." This implies that extricating herself from her relationship would be complicated and perhaps time-consuming and she could possibly get lost. She even has to go through "a full-body turnstile." This would seem to imply some invasion of personal space that may or may not have sexual overtones, perhaps even aggressive ones, in trying to leave the relationship.

She's even required to turn her purse over to the security guard. One of the male members assures her that she will get it back after he takes her across the street for coffee. In the dream, the dreamer is mistrustful of this, feeling that the security guard will probably take her personal information in order to track her afterward. These details would seem to indicate not just that the dreamer feels that it's an ordeal to try to end and get out of a relationship, but also that men will still try to control their female partners and keep an eye on them afterward by perhaps tracking or even stalking them, and perhaps the females' finances may be impacted.

The dreamer shared that her partner is a strong person and, while not overtly controlling, has strong opinions about how others should act. She realized as we were speaking that she had had some unconscious and unacknowledged fears about her partner's potential judgment of her or potential subtle pressure on her to conform. She felt dismayed by these realizations, as she hadn't consciously realized or contemplated them prior to the dream or our discussing its meanings for her.

So this dream is letting the dreamer know that she has an underlying fear of losing her freedom in the relationship and being controlled, as well as of being required in some ways not to be herself. This dream triggered a major aha moment on the part of the dreamer that she had not expected. She knew she was going to have to process the information in order to determine what, if anything, she would need to do with it. She felt that some of the fears the dream was expressing were ones that were her own issues and ones that she had had in previous relationships, although some were perhaps triggered by her partner's personality and worldview.

This dream is an excellent example of a dream providing us with insight we had not expected, while also being a call for action. It requires us to process the information and delve into and try to resolve inner issues that we may or may not have known that we had. This inner processing should lead us to know what our course of action should be. Irrespective of the action we take or choose not to take, we should end up feeling more whole and with less inner conflict just from resolving the issues and inner conflicts in some way. And all of this can come about simply from having a significant dream such as this one.

I feel that this dream likely sprang from the dreamer's unconscious, with some content possibly triggered by a guide.

This dream shows how we can partner with both our dreams and our unconscious to grow and unfold personally and to improve our lives.

Dream #38 Interpreted

Water is obviously prominent in all three of these dreams, with the dreamer actually being in the water, which in each dream is a large body of water (a river, an ocean, and a lake, respectively). As mentioned, the dreamer associates water with spirituality.

There is also a common thread running through these dreams of the dreamer feeling separated from other people, including family members.

Given these commonalities, let's look at each dream individually.

In the first dream, the dreamer is in the water (meaning immersed in spirituality). She sees her family and friends on the shore and wants to reach them. However, the current is so strong that she can't reach the shore (or the people in her life), and she asks for help. Can you grasp what this part of the dream may mean?

To me, this part is indicating that her immersion in spirituality may be taking her away and separating her from the people in her life she's close to. She wants to be closer to them, but the pull of spirituality (the current) is so strong that she can't get to them. This is uncomfortable to her, and she wants to maintain her closeness to her loved ones.

She then goes under the water, conveying a sense of drowning. This may mean that she's immersing herself even more into her spirituality and spiritual practices, almost as if she can't help it because it's pulling her so strongly and it may be overwhelming her. Her husband and another person then walk toward her, walking *on* the water as opposed to through the water. This would seem to indicate that her husband and this other person don't want the separation from her because they're coming toward her, and also that they may not want to get into spirituality (because they're walking on the water without being in it). Her husband actually gets submerged in the water up to his waist, which may indicate his becoming interested in spirituality or exploring it for her sake as he gets closer to her.

However, neither her husband nor the other person reaches out to the dreamer to rescue her or pull her from the water, which makes the dreamer mad. She can't understand how they can be on top of the water as opposed to in it. Her dream is revealing that her husband may not be able to bring himself to fully immerse himself in spirituality and that she is on her own with her spiritual practices and interests. This scares her, as she awakens in a panic from the dream. However, she also realizes after she wakes up that she has the option to go with the flow, both figuratively and literally, meaning allowing herself to go with the strong pull of her interest in spiritual matters and practices and flow with them.

In discussing the dream with her, the dreamer told me that her husband had indeed expressed concern about her interest in metaphysics and how rapidly she seemed to be shifting, and had said to her, "You're evolving so fast, I'm afraid you're going to leave me behind."

She then had her second dream, in which she's in the ocean (signifying immersion in her spiritual interests) along with her family (indicating their joining her in her spirituality). They're all playing, signifying an enjoyment of spiritual pursuits, and enjoying themselves. The dreamer's attention is pulled to an "old artifact" under the water. This would seem to connote the past in some way, whether what happens next in the dream is coming from a scene from the past or comes from an old prophecy.

Everything stops and the water becomes still, much like a device used in films to indicate time stopping due to the imminence of something significant happening. She then sees large black ships, and then her family and most of the other people disappear. This panics her, and she searches for them but can't find them.

She then sees someone from her past who delivers a message to her: "Don't you know you are supposed to lead those of us who are left?" The dreamer then sobs.

This dream feels somewhat apocalyptic and may be expressing an underlying fear the dreamer has—not just that her spirituality separates her from her family, but also that she may have to be a leader in future times if prophecies about Earth changes come true and that being a leader may require her to be alone. The phrase that the friend uses, "those of us who are left," would seem to evoke some religious ideas about the "end times," the "rapture" (or "ascension"), or an apocalypse. Alternatively, it could be expressing a fear of apocalyptic prophecies actually coming to fruition and how separating that could be. If the dream is expressing underlying fears, then it may not be expressing a need to decide between her spiritual interests and her family as much as a fear of what the future could bring and her role in it.

The third dream also expresses the dreamer's concerns. In it, there's a large "elaborate" puppet show on a lake that

many people are watching and enjoying with their fami-
lies. Whereas all the other people are able to see the show
by getting closer to it via "various boats, rafts, floats, etc.,"
the dreamer's only recourse to getting closer is by way of
a "surfboard-like skiff." This part of the dream, combined
with the friends she saw on a houseboat who didn't invite
her onto it, would seem to be expressing a fear of being
inadequate or not fitting in or not being acceptable and yet
again being separate from others.

One significant part of this dream is the "puppet show"
itself. This may be evoking a sense of being manipulated or
being a puppet that someone else is manipulating, meaning a
false "show" without substance—and it's an "elaborate" one.
In other words, there's a mass "puppet show" that's false that
most people seem to be buying into. Because the dreamer
isn't able to participate in this type of charade, the dream
appears to be expressing that she's more genuine. In fact,
when I shared this aspect of the dream's possible meaning
with the dreamer, she stated, "Yes to the feeling of being inadequate. There is a desire to participate in and enjoy the 'illusion.'" So the "puppet show" is signifying the cultural illusion
(mindset) that most people buy into but that the dreamer
sees as false. (This scene is reminiscent of Hans Christian
Andersen's fable *The Emperor's New Clothes*.) Of course, in
the dream, the dreamer paid a price for even trying to participate in this elaborate puppet show by being tossed around
and having her nice clothes soaked. The dream is allowing
the dreamer to realize that she ultimately prefers being genuine and that she will suffer if she tries to participate in the
societal or cultural illusion.

So this third dream is continuing the thread running throughout this trio of dreams of the dreamer standing apart from others and feeling different. (Many people who are deeply spiritual or spiritually oriented do indeed feel different from others.)

These three dreams are expressing the spiritual path that the dreamer is on that leads her to feel different from others, as well as to fear losing her husband and family. The second dream is also colored by all the prophecies of disaster and cataclysm and is expressing the dreamer's underlying fears about the implications and repercussions of their coming to pass.

This fear of being separated from and losing one's loved ones is one I have seen to some degree in various clients over the years as they have been newly exploring and opening up to spiritual interests and metaphysics. Often, as we open up spiritually, our paths may lead us in directions that our friends and family do not go in. So we may feel that we're getting further and further away from them. This is a difficult issue that needs to be dealt with. If our spiritual interest is strong enough, we may find it irresistible and then find ourselves more open and willing to deal with any possible fallout. This fear of losing loved ones as we become more spiritual in a less conventional way is a real one.

Fortunately, there's a flip side to this type of situation, in that, as we open up more spiritually and explore new spiritual interests, we often meet more people along the way who share similar interests and with whom we resonate. In other words, we make new friends who share our interests and spiritual orientation. And it's certainly true that the rewards we get from being on that spiritual path are many and quite desirable.

The decision as to whether to continue on a spiritual path and risk losing people close to us is a very personal decision that each person must work through and decide upon in his or her own way.

I feel that the dreamer could be encouraged by her first dream, as it appears to be conveying a message that her husband doesn't want to be left behind and will want to be with her.

It would appear that these three dreams are primarily expressing a fear that the dreamer has (which probably originates from her unconscious), along with some other, more prophecy-like material thrown in that could be coming from information the dreamer has been exposed to. The message about her needing to lead in some way could be coming from a guide. I sensed that the dreamer would know exactly how to use the information from these dreams.

Dream #39 Interpreted

There seems to be a lot of information in this dream, especially of the symbolic type. Can you get a sense of the dream's meanings?

I feel that it's important to start by parsing out the meanings of the symbols, since the dream seems to be heavily symbolic. The most prominent symbols would appear to be eggs, fertilized eggs, rooster nesting, and men getting pregnant. One common theme running through these symbols would appear to be pregnancy or new life. Another theme would appear to be males getting pregnant or nesting, which is, of course, an improbability in real life.

If the eggs were symbolic, what do you feel they would mean? If they stand for new life, they could be pointing to a new project in the dreamer's life. Intuitively, I felt that this was the relevant meaning. As mentioned earlier, the dreamer shared that she had two work projects going on.

I feel that the first dream especially is giving her some information on these projects. You'll note that in that dream a rooster is nesting and had laid two eggs, which were fertilized, but the rooster had broken (ruined) one of them from lying on it. Meaning?

I feel that this dream is indicating that a man may be in charge of one of the projects, which was fertile and thus promising. However, the man had bungled it in some way (symbolized by the rooster having broken one egg). There's still some potential with this project, as one egg is left, but it will be important that it's nurtured with a less heavy hand for it to mature successfully. Interestingly, the dreamer wrote that the rooster had broken one egg from "laying" on it (instead of "lying" on it). This could evoke additional meanings. One meaning evoked would be that of the idiomatic phrase "he/she laid an egg," meaning made a mistake (and that the rooster, signifying the men in charge of the project, was/were bungling it). Another meaning could be associated with male domination, via the crude phrase that a man "laid" a woman. This is an excellent example of how one word or phrase can convey significant meanings.

I asked the dreamer about this interpretation and she confirmed that one of the projects "wasn't coming to fruition that men were affecting." In other words, men's influence on one of the projects was problematic and preventing the project from coming to a successful completion.

I further felt that the theme of male energy affecting projects may have also been giving the dreamer a message that she might need to inject some male energy into one or both of the projects—i.e., to be more assertive. When I shared this possibility with the dreamer, she confirmed that she agreed that she felt that she needed to inject more assertiveness into the other project. Even the juxtaposition in the dream of the men and pregnancy could be conveying that message, especially with the implied success of the pregnancies. In other words, in the dream it was men who were pregnant, and the dreamer felt that, even though she was surprised that the men were pregnant, she knew that they would be able to give birth (successfully complete their pregnancies, which were projects).

It's certainly interesting that the dreamer's daughter had the same dream on the same night as the dreamer, with the dreamer noting that this often happens. We've discussed this phenomenon previously, and I shared that I had experienced this with my roommate in graduate school.

Since the dreamer's daughter also had the dream about men getting pregnant, there may be a message for her as well about needing to inject more assertiveness into her projects. Another possible reason for the dreamer's daughter having the same dream may have nothing to do with her daughter having projects, but could speak, instead, to the closeness between the dreamer and her daughter. If they're really close, then the dreamer's daughter could have been intuitively and empathically picking up on her mother's dilemma over her projects. If that's indeed the case, then the dreamer's daughter may have intuitive abilities that she could develop.

This dream is giving the dreamer a message and insight about the projects, cloaked in some symbolism, along with a suggestion about assertiveness. I feel that it's most likely coming from the dreamer's unconscious, especially with all the symbolism. Overall, it's quite a useful dream for the dreamer!

Dream #40 Interpreted

There seems to be a theme in this dream of females being used or assaulted by males, with the males assuming they can control or overpower the females and toy with them. The dream takes place in a huge mansion, which may signify an expansive or expanded mind and, interestingly, seems to speak of the dreamer as having a more expanded mind and moving away from male domination or the assumption that males can always control females. In dialogue with the dreamer, I asked if this resonated and she indeed confirmed this.

In the dream, the dreamer stands up to the men as an equal and ends up overpowering them. This may signify that the dreamer has had challenges in moving forward on her path in life, whether due to male domination or the assumption that the status quo will prevail and squelch individuals. Her dream, however, is giving her the message that she can now assert herself and stand up to those seemingly more powerful and that she will prevail.

When I shared this possible meaning with the dreamer, she shared that the personal development course she had just completed was designed to remove personal blocks and teach students to achieve goals in their lives. So her dream represented a confirmation of what she had learned and worked on in the course and signaled that she would be able to stand up for herself and move forward in her life. The part of the dream in which the dreamer put the fire out may also allude to her capabilities in figuratively putting fires out (handling problematic situations).

I feel that this dream probably stemmed from the dreamer's unconscious. It appears to be a dream that is expressing the dreamer's new insight and shift in awareness. Its timing is quite interesting, when you consider that the dreamer had just completed the personal development course. In all likelihood, the course triggered the dreamer realizing that she had felt blocked and why, and her dream expressed and cemented this realization for her, allowing her to know that she could indeed move forward now in her life. What a wonderful dream!

Given that the dream was primarily giving her a confirmation, it would appear that no follow-up would be necessary.

Dream #41 Interpreted

This is yet another example of needing to dialogue with the dreamer to obtain more information.

As it turned out, the dreamer, Jimelle Suzanne, had wanted to write for many years. She had completed her first book, *Blue Vision,* which is a spiritual novel, in 1990, but had struggled to get it published. She had contacted publishers and received about eighty rejections. At the time that she had this dream, in 2009, she had pretty much given up on getting her book published. As she shared with me, "I remember feeling completely exhausted and hopeless one night about writing in order to become a published author. I fell asleep asking for guidance." She then had this dream.

She shared that this dream had encouraged her. In 2010, a friend volunteered to help her self-publish her book, and in April of 2013, this dream became a reality and her first novel, *Blue Vision,* was made available as an ebook on Amazon.

Ms. Suzanne feels that her father, who passed away in 1997, did indeed appear to her in her dream and was trying to encourage her not to give up on seeing her writing in print. She shared that "I feel as though his words and the picture he showed me of my books stacked up on a table were meant to give me courage. It did just that. Every time I start to feel depressed about the struggle with the publishing and selling of my book, his voice flashes back into my mind. It gives me a warm feeling and I know I can keep trying!"

This dream perfectly illustrates how a passed-on loved one can not only visit with us in the dream state but also give us a wonderfully encouraging message that can have bearing on our path in life. You'll note that Ms. Suzanne also incubated this dream, as she had asked for guidance before falling asleep. As a result, she received not just guidance but also encouragement. For Ms. Suzanne, this encouragement had to do with her creative pursuits. As a result of having had this dream, she now has seen her spiritual novel, the first in a series she is planning, available on Amazon and is continuing to write.

Dream #42 Interpreted
This dream exemplifies how much information even a short dream can contain and is yet another example of the importance of dialoguing with the dreamer in order

to extract the full meanings contained in a dream. Even without input from the dreamer, one could sense from this dream that there was an issue with the dreamer's mother and that her mother wanted to be the center of attention (since she was played by Meryl Streep, a contemporary actress considered to be one of the best). These meanings pale, however, compared to the full extent of the meanings gleaned from conversation with the dreamer.

Dialoguing with the dreamer revealed that she had indeed had lifelong issues with her mother, which had led to a breaking of any regular communication with her in real life about fifteen years before she had this dream.

The dreamer shared that she loved to soak in the bathtub. The fact that the bathtub was also a bedroom underscores the dreamer's sense of enjoyment in the first part of the dream, because a bedroom is larger than a typical bathtub. Even her use of the word "drained," when she reported that she had drained the water, evokes her feeling drained by her mother and possibly also drained of any feelings for her mother. Her statement referring to her mother as "a woman I assumed was my mother" evokes the sense that she felt that her mother was not a true, nurturing mother, but one who "assumed" the role of mother or who the dreamer had to "assume" was her mother because there was no other obvious indication (through nurturing or love) that that was truly the case.

The detail of her mother being dressed in crabgrass green also turned out to be significant, because the dreamer said that she felt that crabgrass green was "sickly" and "not a very healing color. As if once was healthy and lovely, now faded and weathered." In other words, for the dreamer this color had the connotation of not being healthy and of being "faded or weathered." So she associated her mother with non-healing things, although the faded color could indicate that her mother's effect on her had lessened somewhat. The fact that she wore "'70s-style" clothing evokes the fact that the dreamer grew up in the '70s and was most affected by her mother then.

The fact that her mother was played by Meryl Streep turned out to have at least two significant meanings. The dreamer shared, first of all, that her mother was "quite the actress" and wanted to be the center of attention to the extent that the dreamer felt that for her mother, everything was about her (her mother). In other words, the dreamer felt that her mother was, at the very least, self-absorbed. Given Meryl Streep's expertise and reputation as an excellent actor, this further connotes that the dreamer's mother was a diva. Another significance of Meryl Streep was that the dreamer felt that her mother was evil. (One of Meryl Streep's best-known roles was that of Miranda Priestly in *The Devil Wears Prada*.) When queried about this, the dreamer stated, "To me, she showed her true self: evil. My definition of evil is one whose mission is to destroy the light in another."

One strong message for the dreamer from this dream was that her mother still haunts her, even if her effect on her has decreased. Even if she's relaxing and enjoying herself, her mother still interrupts her or intrudes into her mind, demanding attention. Her mother impacted the dreamer's sense of peace and sanctity. From this standpoint, the dream is giving the dreamer a strong message that she hasn't completely moved past the effect that her mother had on her and that she hasn't yet been able to completely exorcise the negative effects of her mother. Her mother still interrupts her sense of safety and haunts her.

As you can see, the information gained from dialoguing with the dreamer yielded a lot more meaning, details, and nuances than were gained from the initial stand-alone interpretation.

It's likely that this dream stemmed from the dreamer's unconscious, as it would appear to be expressing these issues, while also giving a bit of a status report on them. To me, it's a wonderful example of our unconscious working on bringing us to wholeness.

It's a judgment call as to whether the dreamer would need to follow up on her dream in any way, especially since she has consciously worked on her issues with her mother.

––––––

You've now practiced interpreting some dreams and received input and validation on your interpretations. Next we'll explore how you can begin to work with the information and insights that you gain from interpreting your dreams.

eight

Working with the Information You've Gathered

So what do you do with your dreams after you've interpreted them? Because the information and insights you can derive from your dreams and the experiences you can have while sleeping and dreaming can be so beneficial, you'll want to be able to work with them and apply their insights somehow to your life. There are many possible ways to work with your dreams and even with your sleep state, some of which can be very advantageous. First we'll look at the various types of dreams and how to work with them. We'll then explore some additional things you can do to work with your dreams and sleep states.

Working with Different Types of Dreams
*Sorting Information, Filing It Away,
and Learning from It*

If you have a dream that represents your mind sorting through information experienced during the day and filing it away, do you need to work with it?

If your dream was simply about filing information away and triggered nothing significant for you, then the answer would be no. Remember that you'll usually have a sense of whether a dream was significant or not. If a dream doesn't feel significant, then I would suggest just ignoring it.

If you have a dream that's serving to file away an experience you had during the day that was indeed significant, I would work with it. (You may not even realize initially that the dream was triggered by something you experienced during the day or day before, but just feel that the dream is significant.) How you work with it would depend upon the dream and the information that's given to you in it.

Let's say that you have a dream about someone you've recently gotten romantically involved with or have just met and are interested in. In real life, you're very interested in this person and want to move forward in the relationship. In your dream, however, someone from your past appears. The person from your past was abusive or really problematic for you in some way and in your dream this person appears with a smug smile on his or her face.

You might wake up wondering why you dreamt of this person from your past in the same dream as your new love interest. What your dream may be telling you will depend upon all the details in it and the scenario, as discussed previously. However, let's say that after interpreting your dream, you realize that your dream is telling you that your new love interest also has abusive or other troubling qualities that are similar to the person from your past. What do you do?

What you do with this information will be up to you, of course. However, you may want to review your past relationship for clues to possible abusive or difficult tendencies that you had overlooked at the beginning of that relationship. Once you do that, you may also want to look more closely at your current love interest to see if similar qualities are there.

A dream like this may actually be giving us a warning or heads-up about something we were not consciously picking up on.

If a dream about current events has people, situations, or events from our past in it that were significant in some way, then the dream may be giving us important information. Once we determine the dream's message, then we should know what to do with the information. This entails using our own judgment, of course.

If, on the other hand, you have a dream of this type and it's not significant, then you won't need to do anything with it.

Expression of Bodily Conditions

Whether you work with a dream that's expressing a condition in your body will depend, as I'm sure you can guess, on whether it's significant or not.

If you have a bathroom dream, then you'll most likely not need to do any work on it.

However, let's say you have a dream in which you have cancer, perhaps colon cancer. The dream feels very real and you wake up feeling fear. What do you do?

Since the dream had a real quality to it, you may want to take it seriously and get a physical. Getting it checked out by a doctor should allay your fears and allow you to know what is going on.

If your dream didn't have a real quality to it, it may not have been giving you the literal message that you have colon cancer. This is where knowing how to interpret and understand our dreams becomes so important.

A dream that is expressing a condition in your body can run the gamut from being quite mundane to being extremely significant. Unfortunately, there's no external authority to determine which type a dream is for you, other than someone who is an expert at dream interpretation. It's up to you to determine this.

Message Dreams

As you'll recall, message dreams are those in which you receive a message of some sort. What do you do with this type of dream? Is it one you'll want to work with in some way?

This will depend upon the nature of the message and its significance. If you wake up from a dream and remember a message that it will be sunny the next day, then there's likely not much to do with this dream. If, on the other hand, a deceased relative tells you in a dream about forgotten funds in a specific bank, then you'll likely want to follow up on the information.

You could conceivably have a dream in which your deceased aunt tells you that she's sorry for a long-standing misunderstanding with your mother. In a case like this, you'll likely want to tell your mother about your dream and the message that was given to you.

Let's say you have a dream in which a guide tells you that you could turn an activity you feel passionate about, but which is a hobby, into a career. Your guide also shows you in the dream some ways to go about doing that. With a message dream like this, you may indeed want to review the information given to you and start to see how you can follow up on it and change careers and direction in your life.

You'll want to review the specifics of a message dream for significance and determine which course of action to take in following up on it.

Communication Dreams, Including Visitation

As you'll recall, communication dreams are similar to message dreams. In communication dreams, you have two-way communication.

Just as with message dreams, whether you work with communication dreams will depend entirely on the nature of the communication, the content, and its significance.

Let's say you've been divorced for three years. After twenty years of marriage, the relationship fell apart and the separation and divorce were quite contentious. You've moved on with your life and made peace with the situation. However, one night you have a dream in which your ex-spouse is telling you how distraught he or she is. As the two of you communicate during the dream, your ex reveals to you how bad he or she feels about what happened. You wake up and

224 • Chapter Eight

realize that even though you have made **peace with** what happened and moved on, your ex is suffering. **In a** situation like this, your dream may be letting you **know that** your ex contacted you in the sleep state because he **or she was** reaching out to you. As a result, you may then **want to follow** up on your communication dream and let **your ex** know that you no longer carry negative feelings or ill **intent.**

The major difference between message **dreams and** communication dreams is that with communication **dreams,** you actually have input and are able "speak" **and communi**cate and give and receive feedback and **information.** These dreams may give you insight on the **particular topic** discussed or let you know that a certain course **of action** may be good to take.

Expressing Fears and Desires

Dreams that express our fears and desires **are often** full of meaning, insight, and import for us. So this **type** of dream, by its very nature, may be presenting us with **material** for us to work with. However, we would likely work **in very** different ways with this type of dream, depending **upon** whether it is expressing a desire or a fear.

We'll look at dreams expressing desires **first. Let's** say you have a dream that's expressing a desire you **didn't** consciously realize that you had. It could be a dream in **which, for** example, you're working with animals on a daily **basis by** helping to care for them. You may already know **that you** love animals, but you may never have considered **turning** your love of them into some sort of career. A dream **like this could** give you an aha moment about a new career **direction that** you would thoroughly enjoy, something you may **not have** previously considered. If you follow up on what the dream has shown you, it's very possible that your life will improve and you'll find yourself happier.

Dreams that express our desires, hopes, and wishes are usually pleasant and may be more enjoyable to work with and deal with. They also tend to be much easier to work with than the other dreams of this type—those that are laden with fear—and there may not be much entailed in working with them.

Dreams that express our fears, on the other hand, are not only unpleasant to have, but they can also be more of a challenge to work with. Dreams like this, which may be bad dreams or even nightmares, often deal with one of two major things: either old, undealt-with issues from the past or potential negative events in the future. This is a broad generalization, as dreams about fears could have to do with other things, but these are the two major categories.

If you dream about a negative event (a car accident, for example) and are fearful in the dream, you may wake up fearing that the dream was precognitive. However, just dreaming about a car accident does not necessarily mean that you will indeed have one. If you've always had a fear of being in a car accident, for whatever reason, your dream could simply be expressing your ongoing underlying fear. If the dream truly was precognitive, there's little you could do, aside from making sure you're always careful and cautious while driving.

If your dream was expressing a fear, you'll want to work on the underlying fear. You can do this by attempting to determine the source of your fear and then, once identified, take action to work on the fear in some way. There are many approaches these days to working with issues such as this, from talk therapy to other modalities such as EFT, Regression, PEAT, and Neuro-Linguistic Programming. (A longer list may be found in appendix A.)

However, not all fears may be easily identified and traced back to a recognizable source. Dreams that are expressing fears whose source we can't quite pinpoint or put our finger on may not stem from your childhood. Your fear could be based in an experience in a previous lifetime rather than in the present one. This doesn't preclude working on it, however.

If you have a dream that's expressing an old issue from the past, whether it's from your childhood or another lifetime, you'll also—and especially—want to work with the material from your dream in some way. Unresolved issues from the past, especially emotional ones such as abuse issues, will often intrude upon our sleeping states and cause us to have difficult dreams, including nightmares. Earlier, I cited the experience I had with a client who had regular nightmares. As you'll recall, he had suffered abuse as a child, but had never undergone therapy. There have also been cases of children having nightmares about past-life issues—of wartime combat, for example.

Irrespective of which lifetime they come from, unresolved issues from the past will often needle us, both while we're awake and sleeping, until we find a way to deal with them and begin to heal them. Issues stemming from childhood experiences in the present lifetime can be especially insidious. They will also motivate and guide our behavior silently behind the scenes, usually in self-defeating ways, in addition to potentially distorting our self-image and self-confidence, which is a major reason why it's important to address and heal them.

Your unconscious is usually doing you a favor by serving up dreams like this to you, because it's trying to bring your attention to something that's keeping you from feeling whole and happy and truly in command of your life. By taking the material from dreams like this as a cue and then following up and working on healing the issues, you'll move closer and closer to being happier in your life and have fewer things holding you back.

The key is to take material from dreams like these and do something with it to work on the self-limiting issues revealed to you by the dream content, by entering into therapy sessions and/or using any of the number of healing modalities available to you. (A list of such modalities can be found in appendix A.) Some people may feel daunted or intimidated by the prospect of going into therapy, but it's truly one of the most proactive and life-asserting things a person can do, usually yielding benefits way beyond what we could have imagined or deemed possible.

By working with dreams and nightmares that are expressing fears and by taking action to rework and heal the underlying issues, you are transforming and transmuting the negative into something positive.

This is one of the major ways in which dreams can enrich your life and be a tool not just for your personal unfolding, but also for your moving forward in life, being happier, and finding more fulfillment. This is one of the greatest gifts your dreams can give you.

Creative Inspiration and Problem-Solving

Dreams of this type are wonderful ones to have. Through them, you're basically given the gift of an idea, a solution, or an answer to a problem you've been grappling with. You'll recall that in chapter 3 I shared several examples of well-known artists and scientists who received the inspiration for at least one of their creations or inventions from a dream.

So how should you work with this type of dream? Once you have a dream of this type, it will be rather obvious. If you dream of an idea or the answer to something you've been dealing with, all you need to do is review the information and determine how to apply it or implement it if you deem it to be valuable and usable information. Rather simple, right?

You can also learn how to increase the likelihood of having dreams of this type through dream incubation. We'll be discussing how to do that later in this chapter.

Expressing Personal Issues and Personal Process, and Working Issues Out

This type of dream is somewhat similar to dreams that are expressing fears and desires. However, these dreams aren't necessarily expressing fears and desires as much as they are revealing our unconscious issues to us and sometimes working them out.

In chapter 3, I cited the example of a client who dreamed that he was dressed up as a vampire on a long train ride. His dream was expressing his inner conflict about being on the path to becoming a doctor because it was not the career he wanted. In his dream, no fear or desire was being expressed or felt. Instead, his dream was expressing his inner conflict and his discomfort with the path he was on.

Dreams of this type will usually express an issue or a conflict we have on a deep unconscious level and/or be actually working through an issue. As you'll remember, I strongly feel that our unconscious works on trying to bring our consciousness and psyche into balance. If we have an ongoing issue in our lives—let's say a deep inner lack of self-confidence—our unconscious may work on that issue while we're sleeping and serve it up to us in a dream.

So how can you work with a dream of this type? If your dream is revealing an issue to you that you didn't know you had, you'll want to chew on and review the information shown to you. If you recognize that this is an issue that has held you back or affected you negatively in some way in your life, you may want to find a way to work on the issue and heal it. Therapy can be a good first step, as can some of the other healing modalities I have shared, and you'll find a longer list of them in appendix A.

Dreams that are either expressing or working on old, unresolved issues are a rich source of insight for us and illustrate how helpful our unconscious can be to us. You will especially want to work with and follow up on dreams like this, as this work can be huge for your own personal unfolding and growth, as well as your progress toward a happier and more fulfilling life.

These dreams, especially, are crying out to be worked with in some way that allows you to take the information given you and work with it for growth and healing.

Healing Dreams

Healing dreams are often fairly easy to work with because the content in this type of dream will often point us to what, if anything, we need to do.

Some healing dreams require no additional work, especially if they achieve a spontaneous healing of an issue or problem. When you have a dream that is actually healing a problem for you, there is little to do other than to take note of the dream and what was healed.

If you have a healing dream that is giving you information on how to heal a problem or an issue, then you'll usually want to follow up on it. Take note of the information or insight given to you by your dream on how to heal the problem. Then simply do what was recommended, whether it's a simple task or a series of steps that you need to follow or take.

What we need to do in order to follow up on and work with healing dreams will often be implicit in the content of the dreams, which makes working with dreams of this type so very easy to do.

Psychic Dreams, Including Precognition, Clairvoyance, etc.

This is the type of dream many people think of when they think of dreams being valuable and giving us information. If a dream gives you psychic information, what do you do with it?

As you might guess, that will depend upon the information you received in the dream. With precognitive dreams, we will often not know whether it's precognitive or not until the dreamt-of event does indeed happen. If we then have a feeling of resolution after the event takes place, that's an indication that that was what the dream was about because the wondering about the dream's meaning is now resolved.

So if you have what you feel is a precognitive dream and a similar event unfolds afterward, check yourself to see if you feel a sense of resolution. If you don't, then your dream may have been about something else. If you do, then you can conclude that your dream was indeed precognitive and you know which event it foretold.

What if the information is clairvoyant? Again, you'll need to look at what the information is in order to know what to do with it. If the information can be acted upon and feels right to you, then you'll want to use it and apply it in some way. Let's say you're in a relationship with someone who hasn't called you in a couple of weeks. You fear that the other person has lost interest in you and that you may need to go on with your life. You have a dream in which you see the other person sitting at his or her desk reviewing bills and feeling very overwhelmed and discouraged. This dream information shows you that your love interest has been dealing with a financial issue that has consumed him or her. You realize that this is the reason you haven't heard from the person and that he or she hasn't truly lost interest in you.

As you can see, a clairvoyant dream can give you valuable insight. Whether you follow up on the information in the dream and do something, or even what you might do, will be up to you.

Psychic dreams are fairly common, more common than we tend to realize. They can give us useful information. If you have a dream of this type and the information revealed to you feels reliable, then you may want to follow up on the dream in some way. If the information requires action, then take action. If it's simply giving you helpful information, make a note of it.

Actual Experiences and Exploring, Including Past-Life Memories

Dreams in which you are not dreaming about something but are instead actually off exploring other places and time periods can be rich with material and information for you.

What you do with the information and experiences gained through exploring will depend entirely upon what you experienced. In the two dreams that I consciously remember in which I found myself in other time periods that felt like past lives, I found the information to be quite interesting and rich but did not feel a need to take any further action. That said, I could have opted to do a regression to those time periods. Likewise, if you have a dream in which you're exploring another time period that may be a previous lifetime, you could decide to have a past-life regression to explore that lifetime further.

What we choose to do with information from dreams like this will be a judgment call. So you will need to determine what, if anything, you should do when you have a dream of this type.

Recurring Dreams, Including Serial Dreams

Recurring dreams, as you'll recall, will often be trying to give us a message about something. They could be alerting us to something we need to work on (such as a personal issue), something that may occur in the future, or even a past-life bleed-through (which is what I call a past-life issue that bleeds through and affects us in the present lifetime).

Whether and how you work with dreams of this type will depend upon what the recurring dream is telling you. If your recurring dream is precognitive, there may be nothing for you to do. The dream may simply be serving to prepare you, on some level of consciousness, for something in the future. (In fact, some say that the purpose of prophecy is to warn, as a sort of preparation, as we don't always have the ability to avert some future events.)

On the other hand, if recurring dreams are about something that you can take action on, then taking action in some way is called for. Recurring dreams, such as nightmares and bad dreams stemming from abuse, would be in this category because they're telling us that something we haven't worked on from our past is hindering us. The same would be true of recurring dreams that are about past-life issues. I had a client some years back who had recurring dreams of World War II. As it turned out, my client had gone through the Holocaust, and the horrors of that experience intruded into her present lifetime in the form of dreams. This type of recurring dream, I feel, should be worked with. Past-life regression and other healing modalities can be used to work on past-life issues.

So allow yourself to get a sense of what your recurring dreams are about and what they're telling you, in order for you to determine whether they need to be worked with and what you might need to do.

Spiritual Dreams, Including Awakening or Opening Dreams

As you'll recall, this type of dream pertains to our spiritual life and will often give us spiritual information or actually trigger a spiritual awakening or opening.

First and foremost, it's important to want to grow spiritually in order to follow through and work with this type of dream. Being spiritually oriented and desiring spiritual growth makes working with this type of dream easier.

If you have a dream that actually triggers a spiritual awakening or opening, you may need to process the experience and/or the information and insight you received. If the information stretches your spiritual understanding, this could require some processing time, whether hours, weeks, or months. You will usually have a sense of when the experience has been incorporated into your life by feeling a sense of resolution when you think of the dream experience.

If your dream has given you spiritual information that enlarges or builds upon your spiritual awareness, you'll want to take note of the information and incorporate it into your general spiritual understanding. You'll want to ask yourself how the information you were given in your dream may apply to you and how you would need to change your present spiritual understanding. This can lead you to know how to apply the information revealed by your dream and what you may need to rethink in order to shift your spiritual understanding in accordance with the new information you received in your dream. Information gained from this type of dream could also lead you to do some experiential spiritual work, via shamanic journeying, meditation, etc.

This type of dream is a gift that we are given, and the information or experience conveyed by it can cover a range of topics. You'll want to allow the content of the dream to determine how you need to follow up on or work with it. However you do that, you should find yourself gaining immeasurably from having had a dream of this type.

Combinations of Types

How you work with a dream that represents a combination of types, as you might guess, will depend upon what the dream was about, the types of dreams it represented, the areas of your life it pertained to, and the information that was conveyed.

Once you determine these things, you can draw from the ways to work with other types of dreams in order to apply any information and insights gained from your dream. It's up to you to make this determination.

———

In addition to working with your dreams according to the type of dream you had and its content, there are some more general ways and techniques you can use to work with your dreams. We'll cover dream incubation now, and you'll find additional techniques in appendix B.

Dream Incubation

Dream incubation is a wonderful technique to employ in order to try to produce helpful dreams and can also be used to help you remember your dreams. It can be used to trigger having a dream about something important to you. When we incubate a dream, we're asking to receive information in the dream or sleep state about something that's important to us, whether it's a creative project or a problem we're trying to resolve.

As I've stated before, I'm convinced that our unconscious is one of the greatest allies we could have. It not only works on keeping our mind in balance, but it will also work on problems we have and give us answers and solutions. I realized this through personal experience over a number of years. Whenever I was working on memorizing lines for a play I was in or lyrics for a song I was going to sing, I would often wake up in the middle of the night with the lines or lyrics going through my mind. This led me to realize that even though my conscious mind was sleeping, my unconscious was still working on memorizing the lines and lyrics. (Thank you, unconscious!)

You'll recall that numerous artists and scientists have received valuable information and ideas while sleeping. Because this is a fairly natural occurrence, you can actually groom the chances of it happening through dream incubation. You can also incubate a dream that will heal an issue, whether an issue from the past or a current one.

So how do you incubate a dream?

It's fairly simple. Before going to sleep, you'll want to think of the problem you want an answer to or information on and ask to receive the information while you're sleeping. Similarly, if you simply want to remember your dreams, you'll want to focus on that before going to sleep.

Sounds simple, right? Well, there's another detail that can increase the likelihood of success with this technique. It will be important that you really *want* to get the idea or information. If you don't really care that much about it, you likely won't succeed. Why is that?

Earlier, I stated that your unconscious knows you better than you know yourself. Not only does your unconscious know you, but it also knows whether you really want something or not. If receiving information on a topic isn't really that important to you, your unconscious will assign it a lower priority and work on other things in the sleep state that are more important to you.

So don't forget to charge your incubation wish with emotion and really *want* to get the idea or answer or to remember your dreams. You'll want to do this every night until you wake up with the answer to your question or idea or find yourself remembering dreams. Don't be disappointed if this doesn't work right away, as it might take several attempts or the timing might not be right, especially if it's a healing or problem-solving dream that you want to have. I'm a firm believer that things happen at the right time. We may need to go through an internal process before our question is answered or we receive the healing we were looking for. It should happen, however, at the appropriate time.

Dream incubation can be extremely useful, and you can learn to work with it.

———

As you can see, there are many ways you can work with your dreams. Dreams can give us so much rich material and be a powerful tool that can benefit us immensely in our lives. We simply need to be aware of that fact and be willing to pay attention to them and then work with them in some way.

Next we'll go over some additional recommendations and points to keep in mind when working with dreams.

nine

Additional Recommendations, Cautions, and Tips

As you've seen from all the material we've covered, our world of sleep and dreams is wonderfully rich and complex. Any one dream can stem from more than one possible source and bridge the divide between different types of dreams by being a combination of types.

Our approach to interpreting and understanding our dreams needs to be similarly complex. There's no simple way or even one way to understand our dreams. Looking for one-size-fits-all "universal" meanings will often rob us of the helpful messages, information, and insights that our dreams can give us as unique individuals.

Dreams can be immensely important for us on our path of unfolding and growing. One single dream can be so powerful in its meaning that it can literally change the path we're on and put us on a new and more fitting one. A dream can also instantly bring us long-sought-after healing on an issue or a mending of a pain-filled relationship or other issue we've been contending with.

The insights we gain from our dreams can range from those that will help us in our relationships, our careers, our children, our life path and purpose, our unfolding and clearing our personal stuff, solving problems, getting creative inspiration, connecting with passed-on loved ones, seeing more of our own potential, growing spiritually, and many other areas. Our dreams can also give us profound spiritual insights we might never have conceived of. They can enlarge our sense of who we are by allowing us to glimpse into some of our "other selves"—our unconscious, our higher soul awareness, some of our past lives, etc. They can reveal some of our own potential and abilities, which can then allow us to develop the gifts revealed to us and become fuller and richer in ourselves. All of this attests to the richness of our dreams and how helpful they can be.

Many of us live in a very narrow range of our consciousness—our *potential* consciousness. Working with our dreams is one excellent way to enlarge our consciousness and enrich our being.

Glimpsing into and exploring the deeper levels of our being, such as our unconscious, can bring us many rewards. This is one of the best ways to live happier, more fulfilling lives, by plumbing our depths and doing inner exploratory work that allows us to see what is actually blocking our fulfillment and happiness. This, then, helps us to clear that old stuff and remove those blocks. It can also allow us to glimpse potentials and skills that might have lain dormant and undiscovered within us.

Yes, it's true that understanding our dreams can be somewhat of a complex process. However, it's something that we can indeed learn how to do—and it's so immensely rewarding that the effort is well worth it. Because understanding dreams can be complex, allow yourself to realize that you'll simply start at the beginning and gain more proficiency and mastery as you continue to work at it. You truly can make progress and become more adept at interpreting your dreams. Remember to allow yourself to start at the beginning and have patience as you become more dream-savvy, learning the language and symbols of your dreams while reaping the rewards of their wisdom.

It can greatly help to hone your intuition and use it in order to more expertly interpret your dreams. My book *Intuition for Beginners: Easy Ways to Awaken Your Natural Abilities* is a step-by-step guide to understanding intuition, uncovering your own, and developing it, and it contains exercises designed to take you from the very basics to an advanced level.

Here is a final summary to keep in mind as you work with your dreams:

- Try to determine if your dream felt significant in order to know whether you want to spend time on it.

- Respect your dreams, no matter how bizarre, and view them as a gift.
- Familiarize yourself with the different types of dreams and their sources in chapter 3, as well as the procedure for interpreting dreams in chapter 5.
- Develop your intuition and use it in your dream interpretation.
- Remember that each detail in a dream can be important and have bearing on the dream's meaning—and that one word or detail can either amplify or change the interpretation of a dream.
- Try to distinguish between dreams in which you were dreaming *about* something and dreams that are actual experiences.
- Remember to pay attention to how you felt during different parts of your dream and upon awakening, as that will have bearing on your dream's meanings.
- Remember that any one dream, as well as any one symbol in a dream, can have more than one valid meaning for the dreamer.
- As you parse out the meaning(s) of each detail and symbol in a dream, look for how it relates to the whole dream and affects its meaning(s).
- Try not to glom onto one meaning that resonates and overlook other possible meanings that also resonate (because of the complexity and richness of dreams).

- Remember that symbols in a dream can be literal or figurative and that some can be both literal *and* figurative.
- If you're interpreting someone else's dream, look for what the dream means to the dreamer, not to you. Don't put your spin on someone else's dream.
- Dialogue with the dreamer, if you're interpreting someone else's dream.
- When someone else tells you his or her dream, pay attention to the person's inflection to see if particular words or phrases leap out at you and convey meaning.
- Remember that Freudian slips or seeming errors in a dream account (or when someone is telling you his or her dream) could also have meaning.
- Look for aha moments of recognition as a key to whether dream interpretations resonate or not, whether you're interpreting your own dream or someone else's.
- Remember to look for individual meanings and not generic ones.
- Remember that even short dreams can be packed with meaning.
- Remember to look for puns and plays on words, as well as pictorial representations and metaphors, for meanings, as your unconscious loves to use them.
- Remember that people in a dream could symbolize parts of yourself, as well as some other meaning, and look for the meanings.

- Try to determine what might have triggered parts of or your whole dream, such as recent events or issues in your life.

- Remember that dreaming of people from your past could have been triggered by someone or something in your present that's similar.

- If two different dreams are remembered that run together, look for the meanings connecting them, and if two different segments of a dream don't seem to flow together, look for the meanings connecting them.

- Remember that actions in a dream, including negatives ones such as violence, could be figurative or symbolic and not just literal.

- Remember that some dreams could be about past-life experiences.

- Remember that various types of elements could be combined in one dream, such as precognition of an event with a personal issue.

- Remember to ask if a dream is yours or is for someone else.

- Remember that even scary dreams and nightmares happen for a positive purpose, such as to bring healing, wholeness, and balance.

- Remember that your unconscious is your ally and is trying to bring you to balance and wholeness.

- Allow yourself to revisit the dreams in your dream journal from time to time, and see if more meanings come to you.

- Remember that some dreams can actually trigger shifts within you.
- Remember that you can incubate dreams, including healing ones.
- Remember that your dreams can tap into and express wisdom and spiritual truths.
- If you have intuitive dreams that are disturbing to you (such as precognitive ones about future negative events), remember that you can ask your spiritual guides, the Divine, angels, etc., for how you want to be worked with. In other words, you can let them know that you're uncomfortable with disturbing precognitive dreams, for example, and that you would prefer to have less disturbing intuitive dreams.
- Remember to use and apply the information and insight you gain from your dreams.

I know this is a long list, but you truly can work on these points and learn how to more expertly interpret and work with your dreams.

Our dreams can be a rich source of wisdom, insight, and healing for us. They're a hugely useful tool on our path toward greater wholeness, fulfillment, unfolding, and spiritual growth.

Your life will be enriched by exploring your dreams, mining their jewels, and learning more about your dreaming and sleeping self.

You can indeed become proficient at interpreting and understanding your dreams—and you now have the tools to do just that. You can use all of the information in this book to mine your dreams for all their riches of valuable insights and information and begin to understand and fully embrace all the wisdom of your sleeping mind. By so doing, you may find yourself beautifully transformed by the exquisite gifts your dreams have to offer you!

Additional Healing Modalities

There are many healing modalities that you could use, in concert with therapy or by themselves, to work on any of the issues that your dreams are presenting to you. Please note that this is a partial list and one that is evolving, as new techniques and modalities are continually being created.

- EFT (Emotional Freedom Technique)
- Regression
- Hypnotherapy
- PEAT (Primordial Energy Activation and Transcendence)
- Healing Touch
- Polarity Therapy
- Guided Imagery

- Tapas Acupressure Technique (TAT)
- Bio-Energy Therapy
- Neurofeedback
- Core Belief Engineering
- Touch for Health
- Integrative Release Therapy
- Psych-K
- Orgone Therapy
- Time Line Therapy
- NLP (Neuro-Linguistic Programming)
- Thought Field Therapy
- Imagery Rehearsal Treatment

appendix B

Additional Ways to Work with Your Dreams

As you saw in chapter 8, there are numerous steps that you can employ to follow up on the insights and information gained from your dreams and apply them to your life. There are even more ways that you can work with your dreams, which can have various beneficial purposes other than those of working with the information gleaned from your dreams. Let's examine these techniques, so you can determine if you want to utilize them.

Imagery Rehearsal Treatment

Imagery rehearsal treatment (IRT) is a fairly recent technique that is designed to help people who have nightmares on a regular or recurring basis. This approach tends to be used primarily for nightmares rather than for all types of dreams.

With this technique, which is usually guided by a sleep professional, you write down the nightmare you've had in full detail. After reviewing your nightmare, you then write out a new and positive scenario that changes both the scenario and the outcome of your nightmare. Your work with this technique doesn't end there, however. You then rehearse your new scenario and envision it several times a day, thus "rehearsing" this more positive dream.

Dr. Shelby Freedman Harris, who uses this technique with patients at the Behavioral Sleep Medicine Program at the Sleep-Wake Disorders Center at Montefiore Medical Center in the Bronx, New York (where she is director), has had a high rate of success in using this method with patients. She cited the case of one patient, who had had recurring nightmares of being surrounded by sharks. The patient then imagined that the sharks were dolphins instead while using IRT in five sessions. The patient's nightmares subsequently stopped happening. In a second case, a patient who had had recurring nightmares of being chased imagined that the pursuer was made of chocolate and then ate him (Beck, 2010).

Imagery rehearsal treatment has also shown promise in treating war veterans experiencing nightmares caused by post-traumatic stress disorder. IRT is a new approach to working with any of your dreams that are expressing fears, including bad dreams and nightmares.

This is a method that you may be able to use on your own. That said, there are increasing numbers of sleep therapists who are using it.

Lucid Dreaming

Lucid dreaming is a technique that has gained in popularity in the past several years, and many books have been written about it. It's a method of dreaming in which you're lucid (aware) while you're dreaming. In other words, you know during a dream that you are indeed dreaming. While we may tend to think that lucid dreaming is a fairly recent invention, the truth is that it's been around for thousands of years in the East and may stem back to the Paleolithic era. It's been gaining in popularity, though, since the 1970s in the West.

I admit that I'm not a huge proponent of lucid dreaming. So many dreams have something to tell us or show us and are thus happening for a reason. As a result, I prefer to let my dreams unfold naturally. Additionally, I question whether we get the same physiological benefits from lucid dreaming as we do from our more natural sleep and dream states. That said, lucid dreaming could be useful while having unpleasant dreams and nightmares so as to change and rework them, including the fears they're expressing.

Let's say that you have a fear of public speaking and in real life have to give presentations on a fairly regular basis. You tend to have nightmares in which you're giving a presentation and the audience members are laughing at you. With lucid dreaming, you would realize that it's a dream and change the outcome in some way, perhaps by changing the audience members' response to thundering applause.

Lucid dreaming can also be used in a benign "dreamscape" way to join other people in the dream state in a shared dream in order to communicate with them or do joint activities together, as sort of a shared altered reality state.

Proponents of lucid dreaming feel that it can be helpful for creativity and learning as well. Of course, regular dreaming can accomplish the same thing in concert with dream incubation—i.e., by incubating dreams that give you ideas, help to solve problems, and assist in learning—with great results.

Additionally, some people feel that one can utilize lucid dreaming for traveling out of body and exploring the universe. I feel that we do that in our dream and sleep states anyway, although we may not bring back a conscious memory of doing so. If you'd like to be aware of doing this, then you may want to learn how to become lucid while dreaming.

There are several books available on this topic, including some by the expert Stephen LaBerge, PhD.

Group Dreaming

Group dreaming (which is also called mutual dreaming or shared dreaming) is an approach that takes the act of dreaming from an individual activity to one that involves two or more people. It can entail individual dreams around a similar theme in a group, as well as shared dreams, when more than one person has the same dream, or a variation on shared dreams, in which the dreamers are lucid (as noted earlier).

Group dreaming can be especially helpful when you're looking to find answers to questions or problems. Members of a dream group will try to incubate a dream that could benefit someone else. A group member may share a personal problem with the group, and in the intervening time before the next group meeting, other members will try to incubate dreams that shed light on the member's issue.

Of course, you don't need to belong to a dream group in order to do this. You can incubate a dream for a friend or family member at any time and then share the information you received in the dream.

Group dreaming can also be used for engaging and connecting with others by meeting up in the dream state in these shared dreams. Shared dreams can be experienced either lucidly or non-lucidly, as well as deliberately or spontaneously. If you'd like to experience shared dreaming, you could try to arrange to do this with someone else and then incubate a shared dream with that person. Again, you can share a dream with someone else whether you're lucid in it or not.

In addition, you can utilize this type of dreaming for mass dreams that take dreaming from an individual activity to a large group or shared one, underscoring the sense that on some level we are all connected via our consciousness. Some mass dreams can happen spontaneously, such as when a number of people have similar dreams about an event that affects a large number of people (such as the precognitive dreams about September 11th). They can also be incubated, such as in research projects when a call is put out to a large number of people soliciting dreams about a specific topic.

Group dreaming represents a way in which we can take the nightly act of dreaming from an individual, private activity and turn it into a more social activity or one in which we connect with others. It represents yet another way that we can work with our dreams, especially when we're seeking answers and insight, both for others and ourselves.

———

You can utilize any of these techniques if you feel that they will benefit you. However, they're certainly not critical to your interpreting your dreams and working with the information from them.

appendix C

Knowing Your Whole Self— Befriending Your Unconscious

The information in this appendix was adapted from my article "Befriending Your Other Self: Plumbing Your Depths and Amplifying Self," first published in the winter 2011 issue of *Innerchange Magazine*.

Dreams give us tremendous beneficial insight that enables us to improve our lives, which is one of the reasons why dream interpretation and working with dreams is so important. Another reason why understanding our dreams is so valuable is that they help to reveal our unconscious to us.

Whereas some people may not be curious about their unconscious self, I feel that learning more about our unconscious and being aware of it is an extremely critical thing for us to do. You'll learn below why this is so important and how you can take steps to do so. This step is certainly optional, which is why it's set apart from the rest of the book, but that doesn't mean that it's any less essential.

Learning more about our unconscious and what lies on deeper levels within us is a powerful way to improve our lives. If we want to be the best we can be and live the most fulfilling life possible, it's necessary to explore and know all parts of ourselves, including our unconscious. There are both great riches and potential pitfalls lying within us in the deeper parts of ourselves that reside outside our normal view, and we can be driven by these unconscious motivators or miss out on potential treasures.

Your Unconscious

That unfamiliar part of us goes by diverse names: the shadow self, the unconscious, unseen motivators, drives, etc.—that deep inner part of us that we may only get intermittent glimpses of. Some of us seek it out, while others may never want to have anything to do with it. And therein lies the great irony: try as we might to avoid going near it, it can drive and affect our waking mind and life constantly and impact us in a negative way, regardless of our desire to ignore its existence.

If we truly want to be in the driver's seat of our lives, then acquainting ourselves with these negative motivators and removing their "sting" and potency is absolutely necessary. And, certainly, using the potential bounty within us only adds to our ability to do and accomplish, as well as to feel fulfilled.

Our unconscious is the repository of our hopes, fears, drives, memories, experiences, likes and dislikes alike—and even more. It's also a powerhouse processor of mental operations. Now here's the interesting part: as much as we may feel that we know ourselves and have a solid identity, the reality is that who we think we are—our conscious mind, identity, and awareness—is but a sliver of our true self. In fact, our conscious awareness is the merest tip of the iceberg. Our unconscious is the huge body of that iceberg lying submerged and unseen underneath the surface of the water.

Our unconscious is so huge and affects our consciousness and everyday lives by driving our behavior so much that one psychologist, Timothy D. Wilson, wrote a book about it entitled *Strangers to Ourselves.* In it, Dr. Wilson writes that "most of the mental processes studied by cognitive and social psychologists turned out to occur out of view of the people who had them" (Wilson, p. 5). These mental processes "are inaccessible to consciousness but… influence judgments, feelings, or behavior" (Wilson, p. 23).

What's the mechanism behind these less-than-positive motivators—our "stuff," as we commonly refer to it? Think of them as our fears, prejudices, and dislikes. They're formed by negative experiences that we've had over the years. In order to better understand their mechanism, consider that the way our brain works is by association. To put it another way, our brain is associative. Any experience we have is composed of a myriad of stimuli—what we see, hear, smell, feel, the ambient temperature, what and who else are present during the experience, etc. Let's say we've had a very negative or painful experience and at the peak of that trauma a cat screeched. Because our brain is associative, all the stimuli of that experience are laid down together and interconnected. As a result, over the subsequent years, every time we hear a cat screech or even meow, we may freeze, panic, feel instantly fearful, or be enraged. I'm using a negative experience as an example, but the same is true of positive experiences, such as the one Marcel Proust wrote about in *A la recherche du temps perdu (In Search of Lost Time)*, when the smell and taste of a madeleine cookie immersed in tea elicited feelings of love.

It's obvious from this mechanism that our behavior can be shaped in a negative or positive fashion by what we experienced in the past because of the patterns that formed and are still viable within us.

The same is true of old tapes that play in our heads from negative feedback from our past. For example, if we were consistently told while we were young that we were lazy or wouldn't amount to anything, we will often have this "old tape" play in our mind when we try something new, thereby tripping us up and sabotaging us almost silently behind the scenes.

The part of our unconscious that contains these negative associations, old tapes, fears, etc., can be quite self-defeating, and when it's active, we're definitely not in the driver's seat of our lives. We are more acted upon and reactive than being the actor or being proactive in our lives. And yet these "demons" within us can be "exorcised" through several modalities available to us today—such as EFT, Psych-K, TAT, PEAT, etc. (Refer back to appendix A for a longer list of healing modalities.) There are so many healing and "clearing" modalities available that we can usually avail ourselves of them fairly conveniently and begin to rid ourselves of this self-defeating "stuff."

There is also great treasure and potentiality lying within our unconscious—from dreams, to creativity and ideas, to awareness and problem-solving. The problem, as with our "stuff," is that it may be lying obscured from our view because it's contained in our unconscious. And yet many people have begun to learn how to harvest the riches lying in potentiality within themselves. So how do you do that?

The term "living consciously" began to be used more and more back in the 1960s and is definitely applicable when it comes to our unconscious. We can learn to observe ourselves—objectively—over time and begin to glimpse what some of our "stuff" may be, as well as what some of the bounty may be. And we can do that in various ways.

The simplest and most immediate way to do this is simply to observe our actions and moods throughout the day and on a daily basis. As we do this over time, we may observe that certain situations or people elicit predictable emotional reactions from us, whether positive or negative. These observations can tell us a lot about ourselves and how we may be affected or driven by factors beyond our awareness.

"Going within" through meditation is a very productive way of becoming more consciously aware of what was previously unconscious. It's really just a matter of slowing down our brain waves to a slow enough rate and shifting our attention from what is outside of us to what is inside (which is, by the way, a natural byproduct of slowing down our brain waves and closing our eyes). People who have learned to meditate or slow down their brain waves through other means are often surprised by what they begin to learn about themselves, as well as by the talents they discover had been lying dormant and latent within (especially intuitive gifts).

Learning to work with our dreams is another method of discovering what is within us and discovering its riches. Our unconscious works assiduously at solving problems facing us, giving us solutions and ideas, helping us learn, and bringing to our conscious attention potential dangers (including even unknown health issues). Depriving ourselves of necessary sleep is not just bad for our health, it's also tantamount to shooting ourselves in the foot when it comes to reaping the rewards of our unconscious via dreams.

Tips for Befriending Your Other Self

Here are some tips for befriending your "other self" (your unconscious), enlarging who you really are, removing self-defeating "stuff," and being more proactively in control of your life.

Learn to Live Consciously and Observe Yourself

Get into the habit of observing yourself daily and making note of your behavior and attitudes. You'll want to observe yourself objectively and look for consistencies in behavior and attitudes, as well as inconsistencies.

Identify Old "Stuff"

What drives your behavior? Do you have any old attitudes, mindsets, fears, beliefs, or old tapes that play in your mind that no longer serve you or fit? Are there any carryovers from childhood issues or abuse that you haven't dealt with? As you identify your old stuff, make a list.

Clear Stuff via Modalities and Practitioners

I shared some healing modalities in appendix A that you could utilize. We're living in exciting times for doing this work, as new modalities are being created seemingly regularly.

Identify modalities that you feel could help you heal and clear old stuff and then find professional practitioners who utilize them to help you.

Carve Out Time to Relax and De-stress

What helps you relax and de-stress? Is it meditation, a nice bubble bath, or journaling? Identify one or more and make time to use them.

Pay More Attention to What's Right with Your Life Than What's Wrong

We tend to complain and grumble when things go wrong, often overlooking the positive things in our lives. This is human nature, as we may be hardwired or driven to strive for perfection and clear up problem areas. However, focusing on the negative is counterproductive. Identify the positive things in your life and make a list. Anytime you find yourself upset when something goes wrong, remind yourself of ways in which you are fortunate. If your car breaks down, for example, remind yourself that you're fortunate to have a car and not have to walk or take the bus.

Cultivate an Attitude of Gratitude

Reminding yourself of the things in your life that are going well and ways in which you're fortunate will help you to cultivate an "attitude of gratitude," which will benefit your health and aid your process of healing.

Learn to Meditate

Meditation is one of the best ways to de-stress and begin to glimpse what lies in your unconscious. It also has a long and growing list of health benefits, as identified by ongoing research. There are several different ways to meditate, so identify the one you prefer. I use individualized guided meditation with my clients and students and have an introductory CD available, *A Journey Within Meditation*, which you can find on my website, www.dianebrandon.net.

Allow Yourself to Daydream

Counter to what you may have been taught, daydreaming can be quite beneficial. Not only is it relaxing, but it allows us to glimpse below the surface of our consciousness and even get ideas. We don't want to overdo it or daydream most of the time, but we do want to avail ourselves of its advantages. So allow yourself to daydream from time to time.

Get Enough Sleep

Adequate sleep is vital for your health *and* for remembering your dreams—and your dreams, of course, can help you to peer into your unconscious.

Practice Dream Incubation for Problem-Solving, Creativity, and Learning

Review the section in this book on incubating dreams (chapter 8), and allow yourself to start inviting some to come to you.

Keep a Dream Journal

We covered this earlier in chapters 2 and 5. Make sure to review your recorded dreams from to time in order to gain more insight on them.

Wake Up Slowly

You'll recall that this will enable you to remember more of your dreams and what was going through your mind before awakening.

Pay Attention to What Is Going Through Your Mind as You Wake Up

Lightly review what was going through your mind while you were still sleeping, and make a mental note about it or write it down. Try to do this before fully waking up and before opening your eyes, if possible.

Learn How to Interpret and Understand Your Dreams

Make sure to practice interpreting your dreams and work with them in some way to apply the information and insights gained.

Cultivate Your Inner Voice, Intuition, and Inner Knowing

This is key to knowing yourself, as well as to interpreting dreams. My book *Intuition for Beginners: Easy Ways to Awaken Your Natural Abilities* is a step-by-step guide, complete with exercises, on how to do this.

Learn to Observe in an Objective Manner

Being clear and objective in our observations is of paramount importance in learning to observe and befriend our whole selves. Make sure to be objective and not bring in any preset attitudes, mindsets, beliefs, or fears.

Bounce Things Off of Your Own Intuitive Knowing

Developing your intuition and being clear and objective can lead you to become your own authority, as you will know what resonates and what doesn't. You can make this a more conscious process by asking yourself, "Does this resonate with me or not?" Don't forget to tune in to ask this question so that you're accessing your true and clear inner knowing.

Learn to Separate Out Your "Stuff" from True Knowing and Objectivity

Remember that your personal stuff serves as a filter for your behavior and observations—and never confuse your personal stuff with true knowing. Some of the advanced exercises that I have in my book *Intuition for Beginners: Easy Ways to Awaken Your Natural Abilities* are designed to help you bypass your personal stuff in order to be objective and get into your true inner knowing and intuition.

———

Again this is just a partial list of ways to befriend your unconscious—and, at the same time, a good place to begin.

Your "other self" is hugely important to you and a potentially great ally, *if* you befriend it and know how to work with it. This is definitely an instance in which what (or who) you don't know can hurt you, or, conversely, what (or who) you do know can aid you—and how knowledge can indeed be power!

recommended reading

There are several excellent books for learning more about sleep and dreams. This list is not an exhaustive one. I highly recommend the following books:

Cartwright, Rosalind D. *The Twenty-Four Hour Mind: The Role of Sleep and Dreaming in Our Emotional Lives.* Oxford University Press, 2010.

Faraday, Ann. *Dream Power.* Berkley, 1972.

Luce, Gay Gaer, and Julius Segal. *Sleep.* Lancer Books, 1967.

Rock, Andrea. *The Mind at Night.* Basic Books, 2004.

Van de Castle, Robert L., PhD. *Our Dreaming Mind.* Ballantine Books, 1994.

It's also imperative to use your intuition in interpreting and working with dreams. I recommend the following book:

Brandon, Diane. *Intuition for Beginners: Easy Ways to Awaken Your Natural Abilities.* Llewellyn, 2013.

bibliography

Alleyne, Richard. "Black and White TV Generation Have Monochrome Dreams." *The Telegraph.* October 17, 2008. www.telegraph.co.uk/science/science-news/3353504/Black-and-white-TV-generation-have-monochrome-dreams.html.

American Academy of Sleep Medicine. "Fun Facts About Sleep." Accessed November 24, 2014. www.sleepeducation.com/sleepfacts.aspx.

———. "Sleep Deprivation Effect on the Immune System Mirrors Physical Stress." *ScienceDaily.* July 1, 2012. www.sciencedaily.com/releases/2012/07/12070119 1638.htm.

BBC News. "Lack of Sleep 'Raises Cold Risk.'" January 13, 2009. http://news.bbc.co.uk/2/hi/health/7823599.stm.

————. "No Sleep 'Renders Brain Erratic.'" May 20, 2008. http://news.bbc.co.uk/2/hi/health/7409195.stm.

————. "Problems Are Solved by Sleeping." June 9, 2009. http://news.bbc.co.uk/2/hi/8090730.stm.

————. "Skipping Sleep 'Hardens Arteries.'" December 24, 2008. http://news.bbc.co.uk/2/hi/7796922.stm.

————. "'Sleepless Grumps' Seen in Brain." October 23, 2007. http://news.bbc.co.uk/2/hi/health/7056611.stm.

Beck, Melinda. "How to Tame Your Nightmares." *Wall Street Journal.* July 20, 2010. http://online.wsj.com/article/SB10001424052748703720504575376994152084232.html.

Beckstrom, Maja. "Health: Sleep Deprivation Undermines Kids' Health, Happiness." *Pioneer Press.* March 9, 2008. www.twincities.com/ci_8478988.

Bell, Kaitlin. "5 Signs You're Sleep-Deprived." *Prevention.* Accessed November 24, 2014. www.prevention.com/amisleepdeprived/index.shtml.

Blanchard, Kathleen. "Too Little Sleep Might Affect Adolescent Brain Development." *Digital Journal.* October 9, 2011. www.digitaljournal.com/print/article/312556.

Blue, Laura. "To Boost Memory, Shut Your Eyes." *CNN.* August 28, 2012. www.cnn.com/2012/08/06/health/boost-memory-shut-eyes-relax/index.html.

Born, Jan. "Sleep Essential for Creative Thinking, Study Says." *USA Today*. January 21, 2004. www.usatoday.com /news/health/2004-01-21-sleep-creativity_x.htm.

Bryner, Jeanna. "5 Mind-Bending Facts About Dreams." *Yahoo! News*. April 28, 2012. http://news.yahoo.com /5-mind-bending-facts-dreams-145028046.html.

Cartwright, Rosalind D. *The Twenty-Four Hour Mind: The Role of Sleep and Dreaming in Our Emotional Lives*. Oxford University Press, 2010.

Centers for Disease Control and Prevention. "CDC Study Reveals Adults May Not Get Enough Rest or Sleep." February 28, 2008. www.cdc.gov/media/pressrel/2008 /r080228.htm.

Coghlan, Andy. "Why Do We Remember Some Dreams But Not Others?" *New Scientist*. May 5, 2011. www. newscientist.com/article/mg21028114.300-why-do -we-remember-some-dreams-but-not-others.html.

Cloud, John. "Why Dreams Mean Less than We Think." *Time*. February 25, 2009. www.time.com/time/health /article/0,8599,1881498,00.html.

CrossRoads Institute. "Brainwaves and EEG: The Language of the Brain." Accessed November 24, 2014. www. crossroadsinstitute.org/learningcenter/qeeg/qeeg -brain-wave-info.html.

Daily Times. "Lack of Deep Sleep Raise [sic] Diabetes Risk." January 7, 2008. http://archives.dailytimes.com.pk /infotech/07-Jan-2008/lack-of-deep-sleep-raise -diabetes-risk.

De Gennaro, Luigi, et al. "Recalling and Forgetting Dreams: Theta and Alpha Oscillations During Sleep Predict Subsequent Dream Recall." *The Journal of Neuroscience* 4 (May 2011): 6674-6683.

Delaney, Gayle, PhD. *All About Dreams.* HarperSanFrancisco, 1998.

Dewar, Gwen. "Signs of Sleep Deprivation in Children and Adults." *Parenting Science.* 2008. www.parentingscience .com/signs-of-sleep-deprivation.html.

Division of Sleep Medicine at Harvard Medical School. "Sleep and Disease Risk." *Healthy Sleep.* December 18, 2007. http://healthysleep.med.harvard.edu/healthy /matters/consequences/sleep-and-disease-risk.

Dotinga, Randy. "Sleep Might Help You Solve Problems." *USA Today.* June 10, 2011. www.usatoday.com/news /health/story/health/story/2011/06/Sleep-might-help -you-solve-problems-better/48288324/1?csp=ylf.

Dream Moods, Inc. "Frequently Asked Questions." Accessed November 24, 2014. www.dreammoods.com /reference/faq.htm.

DreamResearch.net. "Frequently Asked Questions." Accessed November 24, 2014. www2.ucsc.edu/dreams /FAQ/index.html.

Dvorsky, George. "How to Stop Nightmares from Destroying Your Sleep." *io9.* October 17, 2012. http:// io9.com/5952296/the-science-of-nightmares-++-and -how-to-stop-them.

Elert, Glenn, ed. "Frequency of Brain Waves." *Hypertextbook.* Accessed November 24, 2014. http://hypertextbook.com/facts/2004/SamanthaCharles.shtml.

Elsevier. "Loss of Sleep, Even for a Single Night, Increases Inflammation in the Body." *ScienceDaily.* September 4, 2008. www.sciencedaily.com/releases/2008/09/080902075211.htm.

Faraday, Dr. Ann. *Dream Power.* Berkley, 1972.

Ferro, Shaunacy. "New Clues to How We Remember Dreams." *Popular Science.* August 14, 2013. www.popsci.com/science/article/2013-08/clues-how-remember-dreams.

Foster, Russell. "Bring Back the Night: Your Health and Wellbeing Depend on It." *The Guardian.* July 13, 2011. www.guardian.co.uk/science/2011/jul/13/neuroscience-biology.

Foulkes, David. *The Psychology of Sleep.* Charles Scribner's Sons, 1966.

Fountain, Henry. "Study Gives Key Role to Sleep in Helping Brain Learn Anew." *The New York Times.* January 29, 2008. www.nytimes.com/2008/01/29/science/29obslee.html.

Gallagher, James. "Bad Sleep 'Dramatically' Alters Body." *BBC News.* February 25, 2013. http://bbc.co.uk/news/health-21572686.

Gholipour, Bahar. "Why Some Remember Dreams, Others Don't." *Live Science.* August 13, 2013. www.livescience.com/38856-why-people-recall-dreams.html.

Gonzalez, Robbie. "10 Things You Probably Didn't Know About Dreams." *io9.* October 24, 2011. http://io9 .com/5852410/10-things-you-probably-didnt-know -about-dreams.

———. "What Is the Most Common Nightmare?" *io9.* November 8, 2013. http://io9.com/what-is-the-most -common-nightmare-1461032988.

Goodman, Brenda, MA. "Lack of Sleep Impairs Emotional IQ." *WebMD.* June 15, 2011. www.webmd.com/sleep -disorders/news/20110615/lack-of-sleep-impairs -emotional-iq.

Gray, Richard. "Lack of Sleep May Cause Obesity by Affecting Brain's Ability to Choose Healthy Food." *The Telegraph.* June 10, 2012. www.telegraph.co.uk/health /healthnews/9321697/Lack-of-sleep-may-cause-obesity -by-affecting-brains-ability-to-choose-healthy-food .html.

Guthrie, Catherine. "The Light-Cancer Connection." *Prevention.* 2005. www.prevention.com/health/health -concerns/kick-these-cancer-related-habits.

———. "Solve Problems in Your Sleep." *Prevention.* Published December 2011. www.prevention.com/health /health-concerns/how-solve-problems-your-sleep.

Hadfield, J. A. *Dreams and Nightmares.* Penguin Books, 1954.

Haederle, Michael. "Why We Need Sleep Even More Than We Think," *AlterNet.* December 8, 2008. www.alternet .org/health/110997.

Hagan, Pat. "Women Who Sleep Less Than Six Hours a Night Are More Likely to Develop Breast Cancer, Experts Warn." *MailOnline.* November 3, 2008. www.dailymail.co.uk/health/article-1082507/Women -sleep-hours-night-likely-develop-breast-cancer -experts-warn.html.

Haiken, Melanie. "How Stress and Sleep Loss Are Shortening Your Life." *Forbes.* July 5, 2012. www.forbes .com/sites/melaniehaiken/2012/07/05/how-stress-and -sleep-loss-are-shortening-your-life.

Harding, Charlotte. "Five Common Nightmares—and What They Mean." *MailOnline.* Accessed November 24, 2014. www.dailymail.co.uk/health/article-52177/Five -common-nightmares-mean.html.

Hardt, James V., PhD. "Alpha Brain Waves." *Biocybernaut Institute.* Accessed November 24, 2014. www.bio cybernaut.com/about/brainwaves/alpha.htm.

———. "Alpha Brain Waves and Biofeedback Science." *Biocybernaut Institute.* Accessed November 24, 2014. http://lecerveau.mcgill.ca/flash/capsules/articles_pdf /alpha_brain_waves.pdf.

Harris, Sara. "1 [sic] Sleepless Night Increases Dopamine in the Human Brain." Society for Neuroscience, at *EurekAlert!* August 19, 2008. www.eurekalert.org/pub _releases/2008-08/sfn-osn081808.php.

Hindustan Times. "Sleep Lowers Sensitivity to Pain." December 4, 2012. www.hindustantimes.com /Entertainment/Wellness/Sleep-lowers-sensitivity -to-pain/Article1-967500.aspx.

Hirschler, Ben. "Lack of Sleep May Be Deadly, Research Shows." *Reuters.* September 24, 2007. www.reuters .com/article/2007/09/24/us-sleep-death-idUSL 2462796020070924.

Ho, Connie K. "Dream Symbols May Reveal Underlying Mental Health Issues." *RedOrbit.* November 9, 2012 . www.redorbit.com/news/health/1112728601/mental -health-dreams-university-of-adelaide-110912.

Hotz, Robert Lee. "Scientists Are Still Searching in the Dark for the Secrets of Sleep." *The Wall Street Journal.* January 18, 2008. http://online.wsj.com/article/SB 120059164111398073.html.

Hurd, Ryan. "History of Lucid Dreaming: Ancient India to the Enlightenment." *Dream Studies.* March 25, 2008. http://dreamstudies.org/history-of-lucid-dreaming -ancient-india-to-the-enlightenment.

Hurovitz, C., S. Dunn, G. W. Domhoff, and H. Fiss. "The Dreams of Blind Men and Women." *Dreaming* 9 (1999): 183–193. www2.ucsc.edu/dreams/Library /hurovitz_1999a.html.

InnovationNewsDaily.com staff. "People Can Learn While They're Asleep, Study Finds." *Live Science.* August 27, 2012. www.livescience.com/22730-people-can-learn -while-they-re-asleep-study-finds.html.

Intelegen Inc. "Dreams and Dreaming FAQ." Accessed November 24, 2014. www.web-us.com/dream/dream faq.htm.

International Association for the Study of Dreams. "Common Questions About Dreams." Accessed

November 24, 2014. www.asdreams.org/subidxeduq
_and_a.htm.

Jenkin, Matthew. "Can Dreaming Help You Run Faster?"
The Guardian. July 31, 2013. www.theguardian.com
/lifeandstyle/the-running-blog/2013/jul/31/dreaming
-help-you-run-faster.

Jones, Richard M. *The New Psychology of Dreaming.* Viking
Press, 1970.

Khan, Amina. "Alzheimer's: Trouble Sleeping Could Affect
Memory Later On, Study Finds." *Los Angeles Times.*
February 14, 2012. http://articles.latimes.com/2012
/feb/14/news/la-heb-sleep-trouble-alzheimers-disease
-20120214.

Kim, Meeri. "Study: The Key to Remembering
Your Dreams Might Be the Blood Flow in Your
Brain." *Washington Post.* February 22, 2014. www.
washingtonpost.com/national/health-science
/2014/02/22/486125e2-9a56-11e3-b88d-f36c
07223d88_story.html.

Lebowitz, Shana. "What Dreams Say About Your Sleep."
Greatist. February 28, 2012. http://greatist.com
/happiness/what-dreams-say-about-your-sleep.

Lemon, Sarah. "Learning to Sleep: Insomnia Carries Many
Risks, Including Troubling Health Consequences." *Mail
Tribune.* May 6, 2008. www.mailtribune.com/apps/pbcs
.dll/article?AID=/20080506/LIFE/805060307.

LiveScience.com staff. "Women Have Nightmares,
Men Dream of Sex." *Live Science.* January 29, 2009.

www.livescience.com/5275-women-nightmares-men
-dream-sex.html.

Luce, Gay Gaer, and Julius Segal. *Sleep*. Lancer Books, 1967.

Mann, Denise. "30% of Workers Get Far Too Little Sleep:
Lack of Sleep Potentially Putting Public and Workers at
Risk." *WebMD*. April 26, 2012. www.webmd.com/sleep
-disorders/news/20120426/30-percent-workers-get-far
-too-little-sleep.

Mantel, Barbara. "A Good Night's Sleep Scrubs Your Brain
Clean, Researchers Find." *NBC News*. October 17, 2013.
www.nbcnews.com/health/health-news/good-nights
-sleep-scrubs-your-brain-clean-researchers-find-f8C
11413186.

McCall, William. "Sleep Essential for Creative Thinking,
Study Says." *St. Augustine Record*. January 22, 2004.
http://staugustine.com/stories/012204/hea_2077070
.shtml.

McCormack, Lindsey. "The Best Things in Life Are Z's."
Pacific Standard. July 31, 2008. www.miller-mccune
.com/health/the-best-things-in-life-are-zs-4374.

McGregor, Jena. "Why Sleep Deprivation Can Make You
Unethical." *The Washington Post*. May 13, 2011.
www.washingtonpost.com/blogs/post-leadership
/post/why-sleep-deprivation-can-makeyou
-unethical/2011/04/01/AFIIxT2G_blog.html.

McNamara, Patrick. "The Dreams of Men and Women."
Psychology Today. September 9, 201. www.psychology
today.com/blog/dream-catcher/201109/the-dreams
-men-and-women.

MedHeadlines. "Chronic Sleep Disruption Leads to Heart, Kidney Disease." March 19, 2008. http://medheadlines .com/2008/03/chronic-sleep-disruption-leads-to-heart -kidney-disease.

Medew, Julia. "New Treatment Stops Nightmares." *The Age.* October 18, 2012. www.theage.com.au/national/new -treatment-stops-nightmares-20121017-27rgl.html.

Medical Xpress. "New Study Analyzes Content of Nightmares and Bad Dreams." January 28, 2014. http:// medicalxpress.com/news/2014-01-content-nightmares -bad.html.

Melnick, Meredith. "Lack of Sleep Linked with Depression, Weight Gain, and Even Death." *Time.* September 2, 2010. http://healthland.time.com/2010/09/02/lack-of -sleep-can-cause-depression-weight-gain-and-even -death.

Mercola, Joseph M., DO. "Unplug! Too Much Light at Night May Lead to Depression." *Mercola.com.* August 9, 2012. http://articles.mercola.com/sites/articles /archive/2012/08/09/too-much-night-light-causes -depression.aspx.

Michigan State University. "Sleep Helps Reduce Errors in Memory, Research Suggests." *ScienceDaily.* September 11, 2009. www.sciencedaily.com/releases/2009/09 /090910114136.htm.

Mortillaro, Nicole. "Saving the Night: Light Pollution a Serious Concern for Human Health and Wildlife." *Global News.* August 2, 2013. http://globalnews.ca /news/748109/light-pollution-cause-for-concern.

Murphy, Clare. "The Science of Sleep." *BBC News.* February 13, 2008. http://news.bbc.co.uk/2/hi/health/7243141 .stm.

MyHealthNewsDaily.com staff. "Sleep Deprivation and Stress Both Activate Immune System." *Live Science.* June 30, 2012. www.myhealthnewsdaily.com/2784-sleep -deprivation-immune-response.html.

National Institute of Neurological Disorders and Stroke. "Brain Basics: Understanding Sleep." *National Institutes of Health.* July 25, 2014. www.ninds.nih.gov/disorders /brain_basics/understanding_sleep.htm.

Newitz, Annalee, and Joseph Bennington-Castro. "10 Theories That Explain Why We Dream." *io9.* July 24, 2013. http://io9.com/10-theories-that-explain-why -we-dream-897195110.

Northwestern University. "Learn That Tune While Fast Asleep: Stimulation During Sleep Can Enhance Skill Learning." *ScienceDaily.* June 24, 2012. www.science daily.com/releases/2012/06/120624135013.htm.

Norton, Amy. "Teens' Poor Sleep Tied to Heart Risk Factors." *Reuters.* October 2, 2012. www.reuters.com /article/2012/10/02/us-teens-poor-sleep-tied-to-heart -risk-f-idUSBRE89115320121002.

Obringer, Lee Ann. "How Dreams Work." *HowStuffWorks. com.* Accessed November 24, 2014. http://science.how stuffworks.com/life/inside-the-mind/human-brain /dream4.htm.

Ojile, Dr. Joseph. "Studying Sleep for Our Better Health, Wellness." *St. Louis Post-Dispatch.* September 10, 2008.

Olson, Geoff. "Not Getting Enough Sleep? It Could be Hazardous to Your Health." *Common Ground.* May 2008. http://commonground.ca/OLD/iss/202/cg202 _sleep.shtml.

Oswald, Ian. *Sleep.* Penguin Books, 1966.

Parry, Wynne. "The Science Behind Our Strange, Spooky Dreams." *Live Science.* November 12, 2012. www.live science.com/24707-dreams-sleep-science.html.

Paul, Annie Murphy. "How Your Dreams Can Make You Smarter." *Time.* January 4, 2012. http://ideas.time.com /2012/01/04/how-your-dreams-can-make-you-smarter.

Randomhistory.com. "60 Eye-Opening Facts About Sleep." August 9, 2011. http://facts.randomhistory.com/facts -about-sleep.html.

RedOrbit. "Enjoy Your Thanksgiving Nap: It's Healthy." November 25, 2008. www.redorbit.com/news/health /1602671/enjoy_your_thanksgiving_nap_its_healthy.

Ritter, Bruce A., and Ryan L. Caswell. "The Hidden Law of Sleep: Why Is It Vital to Your Existence?" *The Real Truth.* Accessed November 24, 2014. www.realtruth.org /articles/090303-001-health.html.

Roan, Shari. "Cheating Sleep." *Los Angeles Times.* March 24, 2008. http://articles.latimes.com/2008/mar/24/health /he-nightshift24.

Robertson, Duncan. "Sleeping Less Than Six Hours a Night 'Doubles Risk of Heart Disease.'" *MailOnline.* May 2, 2008. www.dailymail.co.uk/health/article-1018073 /Sleeping-hours-night-doubles-risk-heart-disease.html.

Rock, Andrea. *The Mind at Night.* Basic Books, 2004.

Ross, Shan. "Lack of Sleep Can Prove a Killer, Reveals New Research." *The Scotsman.* January 20, 2012. www.scotsman.com/the-scotsman/health/lack-of-sleep -can-prove-a-killer-reveals-new-research-1-2067947.

Rubin, Rita. "Babies Gain Weight with Less Sleep." *USA Today.* April 7, 2008. http://usatoday30.usatoday.com /news/health/2008-04-07-sleep-weight_N.htm.

Salamon, Maureen. "Poor Sleep May Make High Blood Pressure Worse." *HealthDay.* September 21, 2012. Reprinted at http://health.usnews.com/health-news /news/articles/2012/09/21/poor-sleep-may-make-high -blood-pressure-worse.

Schenck, Carlos H., MD. *Sleep: A Groundbreaking Guide to the Mysteries, the Problems, and the Solutions.* Avery Trade, 2008.

Science Blog. "Study Identifies How Muscles Are Paralyzed During Sleep." Accessed November 24, 2014. http:// scienceblog.com/55507/study-identifies-how-muscles -are-paralyzed-during-sleep.

Self Knowledge for Creative Personal Growth. "F.A.Q. about Dreams." 2006. www.creative-personal-growth .com/faqdreams.html.

Sindh Today. "Lack of Sleep May Affect Brain's Information Processing." From a study in the journal *Sleep.* November 2, 2009. www.thehindu.com/sci-tech /science/lack-of-sleep-may-affect-brains-information -processing/article42058.ece.

Slashdot. "One in Ten Americans are Chronically Sleep Deprived." March 3, 2008. http://science.slashdot.org

/story/08/03/03/0616252/One-in-Ten-Americans-Are
-Chronically-Sleep-Deprived.

Sleepcare.com. "Take Control of Your Nightmares: Image
Rehearsal Therapy." Accessed November 24, 2014.
www.sleepcare.com/index.php/take-control-of-your
-nightmares-image-rehearsal-therapy.

SpiritCommunity.com. "Frequently Asked Questions
About Dreams." Accessed November 24, 2014.
www.spiritcommunity.com/dreaming-faqs.php.

Stekel, Wilhelm. *The Interpretation of Dreams: New
Developments and Technique.* Washington Square Press,
1967.

Stickgold, Robert, and Jeffrey M. Ellenbogen. "Sleep on It:
How Snoozing Makes You Smarter." *Scientific American.*
September 2008. www.scientificamerican.com/article
.cfm?id=how-snoozing-makes-you-smarter.

Stringfellow, S. C. "Sleeping on a Difficult Problem Will
Help You Solve It, Study Confirms." *Counsel & Heal.*
October 12, 2012. http://www.counselheal.com/articles
/3086/20121012/sleeping-difficult-problem-will-help
-solve-study-confirms.htm.

Tartakovsky, Margarita, MS. "9 Common Questions
About Dreams Answered." *Psych Central.* 2011. http://
psychcentral.com/lib/2011/9-common-questions-about
-dreams-answered.

TeleManagement. "Diagnose Yourself in Your Sleep: Your
Dreams May Pertain to Your Physical Health." July 27,
2013. www.tele-management.ca/2013/07/diagnose

-yourself-in-your-sleep-your-dreams-may-pertain-to
-your-physical-health.

Times of India. "Prolonged Lack of Sleep Affects Brain."
May 21, 2008. Reprinted at http://findmeacure.com
/2008/05/22/prolonged-lack-of-sleep-affects-brain.

Thorpy, Michael J., and Jan Yager. *The Encyclopedia of Sleep
and Sleep Disorders.* Facts on File, 2001.

Tull, Matthew, PhD. "Imagery Rehearsal Treatment for
Nightmares Related to PTSD." *About.com.* June 25, 2014.
http://ptsd.about.com/od/treatment/a/Imagery
-Rehearsal-Treatment-For-Nightmares-Related-To
-Ptsd.htm.

Turner, Rebecca. "Mutual Dreaming: Is Group Dreaming
Possible?" *World of Lucid Dreaming.* Accessed November
24, 2014. www.world-of-lucid-dreaming.com/mutual
-dreaming.html.

Ullman, Montague, MD, and Stanley Krippner, PhD.,
with Alan Vaughan. *Dream Telepathy: Experiments in
Nocturnal Extrasensory Perception.* Macmillan, 1973.

United Press International. "Study Finds Brain Changes
During Sleep." October 7, 2010. www.upi.com/Science
_News/2010/10/07/Study-finds-brain-changes-during
-sleep/UPI-16291286489350.

University Hospitals. "Lack of Sleep Found to Be a New
Risk Factor for Aggressive Breast Cancers." August 24,
2012. www.uhhospitals.org/about/media-news-room
/current-news/2012/08/lack-of-sleep-found-to-be-a
-new-risk-factor-for-aggressive-breast-cancers.

University of Chicago Medical Center. "Even Your Fat Cells Need Sleep, According to New Research." *Science Codex.* October 15, 2012. www.sciencecodex.com /even_your_fat_cells_need_sleep_according_to_new _research-100197.

University of Chicago Medicine. "Sleep Loss Boosts Appetite, May Encourage Weight Gain." December 6, 2004. www.uchospitals.edu/news/2004/20041206 -sleep.html.

University of Toronto. "How Muscles Are Paralyzed During Sleep: Finding May Suggest New Treatments for Sleep Disorders." *ScienceDaily.* July 17, 2012. www.sciencedaily.com/releases/2012/07/12071113 1030.htm.

USA Today. "Sleep Essential for Creative Thinking, Study Says." January 21, 2004. www.usatoday.com/news /health/2004-01-21-sleep-creativity_x.htm.

Van de Castle, Robert L., PhD. *Our Dreaming Mind.* Ballantine Books, 1994.

WebMD.com. "Nightmares in Adults," Accessed November 24, 2014. www.webmd.com/sleep-disorders/guide /nightmares-in-adults.

———. "Sleep and Depression." August 21, 2014. www.webmd.com/depression/guide/depression -sleep-disorder.

Wilson, Timothy D. *Strangers to Ourselves: Discovering the Adaptive Unconscious.* Belknap Press, 2002.

Wise, Anna. *The High-Performance Mind: Mastering Brainwaves for Insight, Healing, and Creativity.* G. P. Putnam's Sons, 1995.

Wolchover, Natalie. "How to 'Cram' While Sleeping." Mother Nature Network. July 3, 2012. *Live Science.* www.livescience.com/34048-sleep-learning.html.

Intuition

For Beginners

Easy Ways to Awaken Your Natural Abilities

DIANE BRANDON

Intuition for Beginners
Easy Ways to Awaken Your Natural Abilities
DIANE BRANDON

Have you ever known who was calling when the phone rang? Or have you ever made a decision on an absolute whim—and later felt that you made the right choice? Perhaps you've had an immediate good or bad feeling about a person—and then had that instinct confirmed? Most people, whether they acknowledge it or not, have some degree of intuitive ability.

Diane Brandon has spent the past two decades studying and intuitive development. Whether your intuition is naturally accessible or hidden, this comprehensive and approachable text offers strategies to elevate your level of conscious awareness. Dispelling the myths of intuitive and psychic knowledge, Brandon focuses on how intuition can be applied as a tool of empowerment and self-improvement. Get in touch with your inner voice to improve relationships, solve problems, make well-timed decisions, and more.

978-0-7387-3335-7, 312 pp., 5 ³/₁₆ x 8   **$14.99**